REMARRIAGE AFTER DIVORCE

THREE VIEWS **IN TODAY'S CHURCH**

Books in the Counterpoints Series

Church Life

Exploring Theology

REMARRIAGE AFTER DIVORCE

THREE VIEWS

IN TODAY'S CHURCH

- Gordon J. Wenham
- William A. Heth
- Craig S. Keener

- **Mark L. Strauss** *general editor*
- **Paul E. Engle** *series editor*

ZONDERVAN

Remarriage after Divorce in Today's Church
Copyright © 2006 by Mark L. Strauss, Gordon J. Wenham, William A. Heth,
and Craig S. Keener

Requests for information should be addressed to:

Zondervan, 3900 *Sparks Dr. SE, Grand Rapids, Michigan 49546*

Library of Congress Cataloging-in-Publication Data

Wenham, Gordon J.
    Remarriage after divorce in today's church : 3 views / Gordon J. Wenham, William
A. Heth, Craig S. Keener ; Mark L. Strauss, general editor.
       p. cm. — (Counterpoints)
    Includes bibliographical references and index.
    ISBN 978-0-310-25553-6
    1. Remarriage — Religious aspects — Christianity. I. Heth, William A.
II. Keener, Craig S., 1960- III. Strauss, Mark L. IV. Title. V. Counterpoints (Grand
Rapids, Mich.).
BV838.W46 2006
241'.63 — dc22   2005034268

Printed in the United States of America

CONTENTS

CONTENTS

ABBREVIATIONS

BIBLE TEXTS, VERSIONS, ETC.

ESV	English Standard Version
KJV	King James Version
LXX	Septuagint (the Greek OT)
NASB	New American Standard Bible
NIV	New International Version
NLT	New Living Translation
NRSV	New Revised Standard Version
NT	New Testament
OT	Old Testament
TNIV	Today's New International Version

OLD TESTAMENT, NEW TESTAMENT, APOCRYPHA

Gen.	Genesis
Exod.	Exodus
Lev.	Leviticus
Num.	Numbers
Deut.	Deuteronomy
Josh.	Joshua
Judg.	Judges
Ruth	Ruth
1–2 Sam.	1–2 Samuel
1–2 Kgs.	1–2 Kings
1–2 Chr.	1–2 Chronicles
Ezra	Ezra
Neh.	Nehemiah
Esth.	Esther
Job	Job
Ps./Pss.	Psalm/Psalms
Prov.	Proverbs

Eccl.	Ecclesiastes
Song	Song of Songs
Isa.	Isaiah
Jer.	Jeremiah
Lam.	Lamentations
Ezek.	Ezekiel
Dan.	Daniel
Hos.	Hosea
Joel	Joel
Amos	Amos
Obad.	Obadiah
Jonah	Jonah
Mic.	Micah
Nah.	Nahum
Hab.	Habakkuk
Zeph.	Zephaniah
Hag.	Haggai
Zech.	Zechariah
Mal.	Malachi
Matt.	Matthew
Mark	Mark
Luke	Luke
John	John
Acts	Acts
Rom.	Romans
1–2 Cor.	1–2 Corinthians
Gal.	Galatians
Eph.	Ephesians
Phil.	Philippians
Col.	Colossians
1–2 Thess.	1–2 Thessalonians
1–2 Tim.	1–2 Timothy
Titus	Titus
Phlm.	Philemon
Heb.	Hebrews
Jas.	James
1–2 Pet.	1–2 Peter
1–2–3 John	1–2–3 John
Jude	Jude
Rev.	Revelation
Sir.	Sirach/Ecclesiasticus

OTHER ANCIENT TEXTS

Ages.	*Agesilaus* (Plutarch)
Ant.	*Jewish Antiquities* (Josephus)
b. Nid.	*Niddah* (Babylonian Talmud)
Demon.	*Ad Demonicum (Or. 1)* (Isocrates)
Hom. 1 Cor.	*Homilies on 1 Corinthians* (John Chrysostom)
Inst.	*Institutio oratoria* (Quintilian)
Lev. Rab.	*Leviticus Rabbah*
Mor.	*Moralia* (Plutarch)
Rhet.	*Rhetorica* (Aristotle)
Rhet. Her.	*Rhetorica ad Herennium*
Sat.	*Satyricon* (Petronius)
Spec. Laws	*On the Special Laws* (Philo)
ʾAbot R. Nat.	*ʾAbot de Rabbi Nathan*
m. ʾAbot	*ʾAbot* (Mishnah)
m. Giṭ.	*Giṭṭin* (Mishnah)
m. Ketub.	*Ketubbot* (Mishnah)
Pesiq. Rab.	*Pesiqta Rabbati*
Sifre Deut.	*Sifre Deuteronomy* (midrash)
t. Ketub.	*Ketubbot* (Tosefta)
y. Soṭah	*Soṭah* (Jerusalem Talmud)
11QT	*Temple Scroll* from Qumran Cave 11
CD	Cairo Genizah copy of the *Damascus Document*

JOURNALS, PERIODICALS, REFERENCE WORKS, SERIES

AB	Anchor Bible
AThR	*Anglican Theological Review*
BSac	*Bibliotheca sacra*
CBQ	*Catholic Biblical Quarterly*
Chm	*Churchman*
Colloq	*Colloquium*
CPJ	*Corpus papyrorum judaicorum*
ExpTim	*Expository Times*
GNS	*Good News Studies*
HS	*Hebrew Studies*
ICC	International Critical Commentary
Int	*Interpretation*
JBL	*Journal of Biblical Literature*
JETS	*Journal of the Evangelical Theological Society*

JJS	*Journal of Jewish Studies*
JSNT	*Journal for the Study of the New Testament*
JSNTSup	JSNT Supplement Series
JSOTSup	JSOT Supplement Series
NAC	New American Commentary
NCBC	New Cambridge Bible Commentary
NICNT	New International Commentary on the New Testament
NIGTC	New International Greek Testament Commentary
NTS	*New Testament Studies*
P. Grenf.	B. P. Grenfell, *An Alexandrian Erotic Fragment and Other Papyri, Chiefly Ptolemaic* (Oxford, 1896)
SBJT	*Southern Baptist Journal of Theology*
SBL	Society of Biblical Literature
ScrHier	Scripta hierosolymitana
TJ	*Trinity Journal*
TNTC	Tyndale New Testament Commentaries
TSAJ	Texte und Studien zum antiken Judentum
VT	*Vetus Testamentum*

GENERAL

AD	*anno Domini* (in the year of [our] Lord)
BC	before Christ
ca.	*circa* (around, about, approximately)
cf.	*confer,* compare
ch(s).	chapter(s)
ed(s).	editor(s), edited by
e.g.	*exempli gratia,* for example
esp.	especially
ibid.	*ibidem,* in the same place
i.e.	*id est,* that is
lit.	literally
n.	note
NS	new series
p(p).	page(s)
passim	here and there
v(v).	verse(s)

ARE CINDY AND BOB
IN YOUR CHURCH?

Mark L. Strauss

The young woman sat across from me in my office, tears streaming down her face as she poured out her story. Cindy had first met Bob at a church function, and they had hit it off immediately. He was active in the church, and they seemed to have similar interests and values. Eleven months later, they were married. Things went well for the first few years, but then Bob began to grow distant. He was no longer affectionate and spent most of his evenings watching TV or going out with his friends. He also stopped going to church and seemed to lose interest in spiritual things. She began to suspect something was wrong when he repeatedly came home late from work and made excuses for long periods of absence. Finally, he confessed to her that he was having an affair with a coworker and wanted a divorce. Cindy was devastated and tried to convince him to go for counseling. But he was adamant that the relationship was over, and after moving out, he filed for divorce.

After the divorce Cindy remained single for five years, but eventually she started attending a singles group at a church near her home. There she met Dave. Dave's wife had died of cancer seven years earlier, and he had just begun to contemplate another relationship. Cindy continued to attend Dave's church, and the relationship grew serious. She went to her new pastor and spoke about the relationship and about her hopes for marriage. The pastor told her that, while he believed her divorce was justified according to Jesus' teaching, he could not remarry her because to do so was forbidden in Scripture. He referred her to the letter of 1 Corinthians, where Paul wrote that "a wife must not separate from her husband. But if she does, she must remain unmarried or else be reconciled to her husband" (1 Cor. 7:10–11). Cindy was devastated. She wanted to serve God with her life and to be faithful to his commands. If this meant that she was to remain single, then so be it. But was this really what God desired?

Cindy's story is certainly not unique. Change the names and the scenario a bit, and similar stories play out daily in families and churches across the United States and around the world. The issues of divorce and remarriage are some of the most painful and divisive in the church today. I once saw a cartoon by Larry Thomas in a Christian leadership journal, which showed a pastor standing in front of his congregation wearing a full suit of medieval armor (see page 13). The caption read, "My sermon this morning is entitled 'Divorce and Remarriage Among Christians.'" Pastors who teach on this topic are likely to take hits—no matter which side they take.

So what does the Bible say about divorce and remarriage? There are many complex questions and few easy answers: Is it ever acceptable for a Christian to divorce? If so, what are the grounds for a legitimate divorce? Adultery? Desertion? Physical or emotional abuse? If a divorce does take place, what are the options for remarriage? Is remarriage forbidden, or is it acceptable as long as there were legitimate grounds for the divorce? What about cases where there were no such grounds? Does the impossibility of reconciliation (due to the death or remarriage of a spouse) or the passage of time open the possibility for remarriage? A whole new set of questions arises concerning how the church should respond to those who have been divorced and remarried, and whether divorce and remarriage disqualify a person from church leadership or even membership.

These questions are not new ones. The rabbis and teachers of Jesus' day raised similar questions and debated the legitimacy or illegitimacy of divorce. In Matthew 19, some Pharisees came to Jesus and asked him, "Is it lawful for a man to divorce his wife for any and every reason?" (Matt. 19:3). The question

"My sermon this morning is entitled
'Divorce and Remarriage Among Christians.'"

reflected a lively debate among the religious leaders of Jesus' day. Some, following the stricter interpretation of the rabbi Shammai, claimed that divorce and remarriage were acceptable only in the case of adultery. The more lenient interpretation of the rabbi Hillel claimed that divorce was acceptable for almost any reason, even as trivial an offense as burning a meal. A century later, the famous rabbi Akiba went even further, allowing for divorce if a man found a more attractive woman to marry! Surprisingly, all of these teachers appealed to the same passage of Scripture (something that happens today as well). Deuteronomy 24:1 reads, "If a man marries a woman who becomes displeasing to him because he finds something indecent about her, and he writes her a certificate of divorce, gives it to her and sends her from his house ..."

As you read further in this passage, it is obvious that its purpose is not to set out justification for divorce but to prevent remarriage to a first partner after a second marriage and divorce (vv. 2–4; the possible reasons for this will be discussed later in this book). But because little else is said in the Hebrew Scriptures concerning divorce, the rabbis appealed to this verse for their judicial pronouncements. Those who took a stricter view stressed the phrase "he finds something indecent about her" and argued that "indecent" meant "adultery." Others stressed the phrase "becomes displeasing to him" and broadened the grounds to *anything* that displeased the husband.

Jesus clearly rejected a lenient and cavalier attitude toward divorce (Matt. 5:31–32; 19:8–9). But how far did he go in forbidding remarriage? The rabbis almost universally assumed remarriage was acceptable after a (legitimate) divorce. But what about Jesus? Did he accept remarriage as a given, or did he raise the bar and forbid it? Those who claim the former assert that in Jesus' day a legitimate divorce always meant freedom to remarry, and so Jesus must have meant this. Those who claim the latter point out that Jesus raised the bar elsewhere with reference to the law's standards—teaching that anger is equivalent to murder, and lust to adultery (Matt. 5:21–22, 27–28)—and so it is likely he did the same with reference to divorce and remarriage.

The early church tended to follow a stricter interpretation of Jesus' words. Most of the church fathers (the generation of leaders after the apostles) allowed separation but not divorce in the case of adultery. They also forbade remarriage in any case except the death of a spouse.[1] Those who hold a stricter interpretation today tend to point to this example, noting that the church fathers were closer to Jesus and the New Testament writers than we are and so were in a better position to understand his teaching. Those who hold to a more permissive view argue that the early church very quickly lost touch with its Jewish roots, and so misunderstood the fact that Jesus would have *assumed* remarriage was acceptable in the case of adultery. He did not need to state it because his Jewish audience would have assumed it.[2]

The church, of course, has never been completely uniform in its perspective, and at least one early church father, Ambrosiaster (late fourth century), allowed remarriage after a divorce caused by adultery. The Protestant Reformers, too, adopted a more lenient attitude based on their reading of Scripture. Reacting against the Roman Catholic teaching that marriage is an indissoluble sacrament, the Reformers generally allowed remarriage after divorce in the case of adultery or desertion. The Roman Catholic Church in response held firmly to the doctrine of the dissolubility of marriage but tended toward greater allowance for annulment, i.e., ruling that the marriage was never a true one, and so could be made void.

This book presents three different views on remarriage after divorce:

1. remarriage is never acceptable after divorce;
2. remarriage is acceptable after divorce if the injured party had legitimate grounds for divorce (i.e., adultery or desertion); and
3. remarriage is potentially acceptable also for abuse.

All three of the contributors are renowned and respected biblical scholars, experts in the biblical languages and cultures of the Old and New Testaments. Each has done extensive research and writing in the area of divorce and remarriage. All three are also friends who are able to discuss these issues in a balanced and irenic manner with a true spirit of Christian love. Each also has a pastor's heart. Their passion is to build up the church, the body of Christ, and to help it to be all that God wants it to be.

They write not only for church leaders and students but also for concerned lay Christians who may be facing this issue in their own lives or may want to help affected family members or friends in their church. This book is written for anyone who could profit from an informed but accessible overview in a single volume covering the range of views held in today's church. The discussion will not only open up Scripture but also apply it to some of the practical issues that affect church life. The discussion questions are designed to be used for those who want to use this book in classroom or small group settings.

I hope you will approach this book not as a debate, with winners and losers, but as a dialogue, a conversation that will provide the church with greater wisdom and insight concerning this complex topic. Please do not read simply to justify your own position or to get ammunition to attack other views. Instead, keep an open mind and learn from each position, seeking to discern the mind of Christ. Remarriage after divorce is never merely an academic issue, considered without emotion or passion. Divorce is always painful and damaging, involving the breaking of a sacred covenant before God and a shattering of the most intimate kind of human relationship. The topic can never be discussed without emotions. Yet we can sanctify these emotions by always keeping in mind the fundamental mandate of the Christian life: loving God with our heart, soul, strength, and mind, and loving our neighbors as ourselves (Matt. 22:36–40). Keep this attitude in mind as you read this book, seeking to discern the mind of Christ and God's will for your life (1 Cor. 2:16).

Introduction: Are Cindy and Bob in Your Church?

1. Even remarriage after one's spouse died was frowned on by many. See Michael Gorman, "Divorce and Remarriage from Augustine to Zwingli," *Christianity Today* 36 (December 14, 1992): 30–31.

2. See David Instone-Brewer, *Divorce and Remarriage in the Bible: The Social and Literary Context* (Grand Rapids: Eerdmans, 2002), 238–39.

Chapter One

NO REMARRIAGE AFTER DIVORCE

NO REMARRIAGE AFTER DIVORCE

Gordon J. Wenham

The issue of remarriage after divorce painfully divides evangelical Christians. Perhaps you have seen tension over this issue in your own family or church or among your friends. I hope to shed light on what I believe Scripture teaches about this sensitive issue. My goal is that you will become biblically informed and feel better equipped to discuss the issue. But before I set out the reasons why I think divorced Christians should *not* remarry, I want to set out some points about marriage with which I believe my coauthors agree. Perhaps you will agree as well.

POINTS OF AGREEMENT ABOUT MARRIAGE

First, the Bible advocates lifelong, monogamous heterosexual marriage as best for human welfare. Jesus points to two passages in Genesis as foundational for his view of marriage (Mark 10:6–7; Matt. 19:4–5). The first is Genesis 1:27–28, which tells of God's creation of man and woman in his image. Their union is blessed by God as a means of perpetuating the human race for the benefit of creation. They are told to "be fruitful and increase in number." The second passage Jesus cites, Genesis 2:24, is even more explicit about biblical ideals for marriage. Adam's loneliness could not be satisfied by the creation of the animals or by the creation of other men, but by just one woman. Adam's joy at Eve's creation shows that monogamous heterosexual partnership offers the most satisfying sort of human relationship. It is noteworthy, too, that Eve is created out of Adam's rib. She is formed from him, which indicates the intimate bond between them—and between every married couple. This is summed up in Jesus' quotation of Genesis 2:24 in Matthew 19:5: "For this reason a man will leave his father and mother and be united to his wife, and the two will become one flesh."

The Hebrew term here translated "be united," which may also be rendered "stick," suggests a bond that cannot easily be broken. Indeed, the statement that they become "one flesh" is a description of the relationship between close relatives (cf. Gen 29:14), which endures whatever changes occur to the related individuals.

The second point of agreement with my colleagues is that marriage is an image of the relationship between God and Israel, and in the New Testament it's an image of Christ and the church. Traditionally, Song of Songs, which on the surface is all about human love, has been understood as an image of God and his bride, Israel, or the church. The prophets identify the infidelity of Israel as adultery against God (cf. Jeremiah, Ezekiel, Hosea). The apostle Paul is most explicit: "Husbands, love your wives, just as Christ loved the church and gave himself up for her.... 'For this reason a man will leave his father and mother and be united to his wife, and the two will become one flesh.' This is a profound mystery—but I am talking about Christ and the church" (Eph. 5:25, 31–32).

The third point of agreement is the understanding that divorce is a failure due to sin. As Jesus put it, "Moses permitted you to divorce your wives because your hearts were hard. But it was not this way from the beginning" (Matt. 19:8). Though *all* of us are sinners, and this fact will have an obvious impact on the marriage relationship, to agree that divorce is caused by sin is not to say that, when it occurs, both parties are equally to blame. Some divorced people are more innocent than others. But when divorce occurs, it demonstrates a breakdown in relationships, which is at odds with the gospel message of forgiveness and reconciliation. God loves us even though we are sinners (Rom. 5:8), so his people should love each other despite the experience and reality of sin.

The fourth point of agreement is the awareness that the present situation is catastrophic. The present anarchy in sexual behavior is leading to family and social instability on an unparalleled scale. In Western societies, about half of marriages end in divorce. A large percentage of children are born out of wedlock. One in five pregnancies is aborted. Teenage homelessness is largely caused by conflict with stepfathers. Violence between partners is five times as common in cases where the couple cohabits rather than marries. Child abuse is thirty times more common in situations where single mothers have a series of boyfriends. The non-Western world is appalled as they look at the West and its destruction of family values.[1]

None of us would suggest that simply banning divorce and remarriage will cure the breakdown of family life. But I believe that the rejection of the traditional Christian approach to this issue is one part of the package of secularism that has led to our present situation. We cannot simply turn the clock back and restore primitive Christian practices in our broken society, but we do need to recapture the biblical understanding of marriage and press our churches and our politicians to change their approach to family issues, so that once again there are incentives for people to follow the Christian pathway.

It is my contention that both the New Testament and the history of the church support the view that Christians should not remarry after divorce.[2] Because this view is so little appreciated in American evangelical circles, I want to spend most of this chapter on giving you reasons why I believe it is the correct view.

MY ARGUMENT FOR NO REMARRIAGE
AFTER DIVORCE

The argument proceeds in four stages (see chart on p. 22). First, I will examine the attitude of the early church. In the first three centuries of the Christian era, not a single writer supposes that the New Testament allows remarriage after divorce. Since these writers' mother tongue was Greek, they understood the language of the New Testament much better than any modern scholar. Furthermore, the very earliest writers may have known the apostles personally—or at least their immediate successors—so they would have been familiar with apostolic attitudes.

Second, I will look at the teaching of the texts dealing with marriage *outside* Matthew, such as Paul's teaching in 1 Corinthians 7 and Romans 7, as well as the teaching of Jesus as reported in Mark 10 and Luke 16. Were we in possession of only *these* texts, there would be no question that the New Testament forbids remarriage after divorce.

Third, I will look at the teaching in Matthew's gospel. Matthew wrote the only gospel that mentions an exception to Jesus' blanket condemnation of divorce and remarriage. In Matthew 5:32, divorce is not condemned as adultery in cases where the divorce is caused by sexual immorality, but other reasons for divorce and any remarriage after divorce are so condemned; the same ideas are reiterated in Matthew 19. Some interpreters interpret Matthew 19 to allow remarriage after some divorces (see the other chapters in this book). I will argue that this makes Jesus contradict himself. The text makes much better sense if Jesus is understood to prohibit remarriage after divorce in every case.

Fourth, I will briefly comment on the Jewish mind-set about divorce in Jesus' day. Here I agree with my colleagues that both the Old Testament and first-century Judaism allowed people to remarry after divorce. I do not think the Old Testament likes divorce or remarriage afterward, but it certainly does not ban them. However, it does not follow that because first-century Jews allowed remarriage after divorce, Jesus did too. One of the fundamental themes of the Gospels is Jesus' conflict with Jews of his day. That is one reason he was crucified. So I find it quite unconvincing to argue that on the divorce issue he agreed with the Jews; in fact, it makes nonsense of the argument in Matthew 19.

When I have established what I believe the New Testament teaches about remarriage, I'll make some observations on how this teaching should be implemented in churches and a society for which it is a quite novel, if not shocking, view.

STAGES IN THE CASE FOR THE NO-REMARRIAGE VIEW
1. Support in the attitude of the early church – first five centuries
2. Support from the New Testament outside of Matthew
3. Support from Matthew's gospel
4. Support from the Judaism of Christ's day

The Early Church Context

Early Christian writers—often referred to as the church fathers—almost universally rejected remarriage after divorce.[3] Among Greek-speaking fathers there was total unanimity. The earlier writers (Hermas, Justin, Athenagoras, Theophilus of Antioch, Irenaeus, Clement of Alexandria, and Origen) all explicitly condemned remarriage after divorce or clearly presupposed this view. The Constantinian settlement that made Christianity the official religion of the empire (ca. AD 312) might have encouraged Christian writers to identify imperial legal practice, which permitted divorce and remarriage, with Christian values. But there was no sign of that happening. Later Greek theologians such as Basil, Gregory Nazianzus, Apollinarius, Theodore of Mopsuestia, and John Chrysostom all maintained the traditional Christian position that the Gospels do not permit remarriage after divorce. These theologians regarded the exception clause as authorizing or requiring separation, not permitting remarriage afterward.[4] That this was the way native Greek speakers understood our Lord's teaching surely indicates it is the most natural interpretation.

The evidence of the Latin fathers is equally impressive. Among those who condemned remarriage after divorce were Tertullian, Ambrose, Innocent, Pelagius, Jerome, and Augustine. There was only one dissenting voice in the West, namely, Ambrosiaster, who wrote between 366 and 383. His views on marriage and divorce were strongly influenced by Roman law. For example, he regarded adultery by a husband as much less serious than that by a wife. This inequality put him at odds with both the New Testament and the general attitude of the early church, which always insisted on mutual fidelity. Little wonder that Ambrosiaster was ignored by subsequent fifth-century Latin writers.

The witness of the early church thus points unequivocally to a no-remarriage understanding of the gospel divorce texts. Since no modern New Testament scholar can ever hope to approach the Greek fathers' grasp of their mother tongue and its nuances, dissenters will have to have extremely powerful arguments to show that the understanding of the Greek fathers is not the natural understanding of the texts.

The New Testament Context (apart from Matthew)

But could these Fathers have misunderstood the gospel divorce texts? Although they were much closer in time, place, language, and presuppositions than the modern reader is to the gospel texts, they were not contemporaries of the Evangelists. So although it is very unlikely that they misunderstood Jesus' teaching, it is not impossible. I'll first examine the teaching of Paul in his letters and Jesus in the gospels of Mark and Luke to see whether they allow remarriage after divorce. Then I will turn to the statements unique to Matthew.

Paul's Letters

Paul's comments in 1 Corinthians 7:10–11 (cf. Rom. 7:2–3) are very explicit: "To the married I give this command (not I, but the Lord): A wife must not separate from her husband. But if she does, she must remain unmarried or else be reconciled to her husband. And a husband must not divorce his wife."

Paul makes three points here. First, his teaching is based on Jesus' teaching ("not I, but the Lord"). This is one of four passages in 1 Corinthians where Paul explicitly appeals to Jesus' own teaching to justify his instructions. Second, couples should not divorce each other. Third, if one does leave the other, she should not remarry. Paul does not actually say that a husband who divorces his wife should not remarry, but this is surely implied. If he should not divorce his wife, he certainly should not remarry.

Gordon Fee sums up the thrust of this passage this way:

There is little question that both Paul and Jesus disallowed divorce between two believers, especially when it served as grounds for remarriage.... On the other hand ... divorce may happen.... What is not allowed is remarriage, both because for him that presupposes the teaching of Jesus that such is adultery and because in the Christian community reconciliation is the norm. If the Christian husband and wife cannot be reconciled to one another, then how can they expect to become models of reconciliation before a fractured and broken world?[5]

The thrust of Paul's teaching may be clear, but it is not so obvious what form of Jesus' teaching he was appealing to. Did Paul know the gospel sayings about divorce in the form in which we now have them in the Gospels, or was he appealing to some tradition independent of them? If it could be proved that he knew the sayings in their gospel form, the no-remarriage view would be unassailable. But, of course, this is not so easy to demonstrate, especially because the critical consensus is that the Synoptic Gospels (Matthew, Mark, Luke) were written after Paul's epistles.

As my case at this point rests not on Paul's knowing Matthew in its present form but only on the observation that nowhere outside Matthew 19 is there ever a hint that remarriage after divorce might be allowed, I will first review the remarks in Luke and Mark. Then I'll reopen the question of Matthew 19.

The Gospels of Mark and Luke

Two cases are discussed in Mark and Luke—the husband who divorces and remarries, and the divorced woman who remarries. I will consider, first, the remarrying husband:

- "Anyone who divorces his wife and marries another woman commits adultery against her" (Mark 10:11).
- "Anyone who divorces his wife and marries another woman commits adultery" (Luke 16:18a).

Despite very slight differences in wording, both sayings make two remarkable points. First, a husband can commit adultery against his own wife. This is implied by Luke and explicit in Mark. But under Old Testament law, adultery was committed against *husbands*, not against wives. If a married man took a second partner in marriage, or had intercourse with her without marrying her, it did not count as adultery; hence, the practice of polygamy was legal. However, if a married *woman* had sexual relations with anyone except her husband, it was adultery by her and the third party. But this saying of Jesus introduces full reciprocity into marriage law: infidelity by a husband is just as culpable as infidelity by a wife. Second, Jesus also implies that polygamy is not permitted. Divorce was supposed to give permission for a second union without the stigma of adultery.

But if a second union after divorce with the explicit permission for remarriage that divorce entailed was to be counted as adultery according to Jesus, how much more second or subsequent unions *without* divorce.[6]

However, it is also important to notice what is not said. Divorce on its own is not equated with adultery, only divorce followed by remarriage. The same is true of the second half of the statement in both gospels:

- "And if she divorces her husband and marries another man, she commits adultery" (Mark 10:12).
- "... and the man who marries a divorced woman commits adultery" (Luke 16:18b).

Luke's form of the statement is almost the same as the statement in Matthew 5:32b. Mark's form is unusual in that it envisages a woman taking the initiative in divorce proceedings, which rarely happened in first-century Palestine.[7] But what is striking about both forms of the saying is the implication that divorce does not break the marriage bond, so that sexual relations with anyone but one's first spouse is adultery.

According to Jewish law, "the essential formula in the bill of divorce is 'Lo, thou art free to marry any man'" (*m. Giṭ* 9:3). The implication of Jesus' pronouncement is that the essential declaration in the divorce formula does not work. A woman is *not* free to marry any man after divorce. If she does, she commits adultery. In other words, she is still bound by the vow of exclusive loyalty to her husband. Thus the two halves of the statements in Luke 16:18 and Mark 10:11–12 place both partners under the same obligations of mutual loyalty. If either husband or wife divorces the other and remarries, he or she commits adultery against the other because they are both bound together as husband and wife.

The theological logic behind this position is explained in Jesus' debate with the Pharisees that immediately precedes these remarks in Mark 10. Asked whether divorce was legal, Jesus declared it contradicted God's creative purpose that in marriage "'the two will become one flesh.' So they are no longer two, but one. Therefore what God has joined together, let man not separate" (vv. 8–9). It is because God joins a couple together in marriage that the human declaration "You are free to marry any man" has no legal effect in God's eyes. He looks on remarriage after divorce as adultery.

My interim conclusion is, therefore, that in the wider NT context outside Matthew's gospel, there is no permission for remarriage after divorce. The teaching of Jesus as reported by Mark, Luke, and Paul is completely congruent with the teaching of the early church on this issue from the second to the fifth centuries AD. This makes it unlikely that Matthew's gospel should be interpreted differently. If it is to be dated as late as AD 85, as is often suggested, it would be curious if its teaching on marriage differed so radically from the NT texts that preceded it and the early church fathers who followed it. On the other hand, if it was written much earlier, as church tradition maintained, why did Paul and the other Evangelists understand Jesus' teaching so differently? Whatever context we prefer for Matthew's gospel, it is clear that the writers closest to him in time understood Jesus to prohibit remarriage after divorce.

The Context in Matthew

So far what I have said is widely accepted. Historians agree that the early church did not approve of remarriage after divorce. Most biblical scholars accept that the New Testament, apart from Matthew, also condemned remarriage after divorce. The idea that Matthew allowed remarriage after divorce in some cases rests on the interpretation of two short phrases. In 5:32 Jesus declared that "everyone who divorces his wife, *except on the ground of sexual immorality* [*porneia*], makes her commit adultery" (ESV, emphasis added). In 19:9 Jesus noted that "whoever divorces his wife, *except for sexual immorality* [*porneia*], and marries another, commits adultery" (ESV, emphasis added). The early church understood the italicized phrases to allow separation, but not remarriage, for sexual immorality (*porneia*).[8] But from the time of Erasmus (1519) on, many Protestants have held that the exception clauses allow full divorce with the right to remarry in cases where a spouse is guilty of sexual immorality, typically adultery. I want to examine which interpretation — the permissive Erasmian view or the restrictive early church view — makes the best sense within the context of

Matthew's gospel and the flow of his thought. I'll look at the two passages in turn.

Matthew 5:32

Matthew 5:32 is unusual in that it says the act of divorce causes the woman to commit adultery. How can divorce by itself cause adultery? The most likely explanation is that the woman will be forced by economic or social pressure to remarry. The husband who initiates the divorce has thereby himself caused her to break the seventh commandment.[9] All the blame is being transferred to the man.

This approach fits the rest of Jesus' exposition of the seventh commandment in the Sermon on the Mount. Contrary to much Jewish thinking, which tended to blame women for sexual sins, Jesus focuses all his attention on the male and the steps men must take to avoid falling into temptation. It is the man who looks at a woman lustfully in verse 28. It is the man who must gouge out his right eye or cut off his right hand in verses 29–30. It is the man who causes the woman to commit adultery in verse 32a or commits adultery himself in verse 32b.

Not only is the focus on the man in this passage, but there is a progression in the seriousness of the man's sin (see diagram below). It begins in the man's mind ("adultery ... in his heart"), develops in his eyes, and then moves to his hand. Next it becomes adultery by proxy ("causes her to commit adultery," ESV), and finally he commits adultery himself by marrying a divorced woman.

PROGRESSION OF SIN IN MAN

Mind → Eyes → Hand → Proxy → Adultery by marrying divorced woman

---

Within this context, the exception clause simply notes that should a wife have already committed adultery—one type of sexual immorality—her husband can hardly be said to have made her commit adultery. There is no suggestion here that a husband gains the right to marry again. The most that permissive interpreters can claim is that this text leaves open the *possibility* that an innocent husband may remarry. This text certainly does not authorize remarriage in such circumstances.

The whole tenor of the passage suggests that a permissive interpretation is wrong. The point Jesus is focusing on here is the man's responsibility to be loyal to his wife. Men must make every effort to avoid transgressing the commandment, even in their thought-life. To see the idea of remarriage in verse 32a, where the central concern is to prohibit men from even divorcing their wives, is surely unlikely. It becomes even more unlikely when we reach verse 32b, where marrying any divorced woman is the climax of Jesus' exposition of the seventh commandment's implications. Contextually, therefore, a reading that allows for remarriage after some divorces in 32a misses the central thrust of this section—its focus on male waywardness—and the way it builds to its climax in 32b.

Remarriage readings also lead to an illogicality in verse 32.[10] Such an interpretation offers a perverse incentive to sexual immorality. For if the only circumstance in which someone is free to remarry is when the spouse has committed adultery, one could envisage a partner in a desperate marriage encouraging the other to commit adultery in order to secure freedom to remarry instead of to merely separate. But this type of casuistry seems far removed from Jesus' approach. In context, he is condemning every kind of infidelity, not providing excuses for remarriage.

This reading of Matthew 5:32 suggests that, far from giving an escape clause from Jesus' condemnation of remarriage found in the other gospels, Matthew could be underlining the strictness of Jesus' teaching against divorce. According to Matthew 5:32b; Mark 10:11–12; and Luke 16:18, divorce followed by remarriage is equivalent to adultery. But according to Matthew 5:32 ("anyone who divorces his wife ... causes her to commit adultery"), divorce by itself can lead to the breaking of the seventh commandment.[11]

I would, therefore, sum up Matthew's version of Jesus' words in three statements:

1. Divorce + remarriage = adultery (5:32b; cf. Mark 10:11–12; Luke 16:18).
2. Divorce alone (except for *porneia*) = adultery (5:32a).
3. Divorce (except for *porneia*) + remarriage = adultery (19:9).

Matthew 19:9

Having established that Matthew 5:32 offers no support for permissive interpretations, I now wish to argue that the same sense fits 19:9: "Anyone who divorces his wife, except for [*porneia*], and marries another woman commits adultery." In his monumental study, Hans Dieter Betz sums up Jesus' teaching in Matthew 19 as follows: "Matthew seems to be affirming … that any remarriage after divorce is adulterous but that divorce alone is not."[12]

To understand Matthew 19:9 correctly, it is important to read it in context and to understand how it fits into Jesus' argument. It comes in the course of a debate with the Pharisees about the justification for divorce: "Some Pharisees came to him to test him. They asked, 'Is it lawful for a man to divorce his wife for any and every reason?'" (19:3). This is slightly different from the way Mark phrases the Pharisaic question: "Is it lawful for a man to divorce his wife?" (Mark 10:2). Matthew clearly situates the debate in the context of intra-Jewish disputes about reasons for divorce, whereas Mark simplifies the debate to bring out the essence of the dispute for Gentile readers. In Matthew 19:3, Jesus is asked to say on whose side he is when it comes to allowing for divorce. Does he agree with the conservative Shammaites, who allowed divorce on very few grounds, or with the liberal Hillelites?

Before looking at Jesus' argument about divorce, we should point out that the pattern of the debate here is typical of many in the Gospels (see chart below):[13]

ACTION	SCRIPTURE
1. Someone asks a question.	Matthew 19:16
2. Jesus attacks the very foundations of his opponents' position.	Matthew 19:17
3. They counterattack, raising objections from Scripture to his views.	Matthew 19:18, 20
4. Jesus dismisses these objections.	Matthew 19:21, 24
5. Then the disciples interject their struggles with Jesus' teaching.	Matthew 19:25
6. Finally, Jesus reaffirms his own position and challenges his disciples to have faith and accept it.	Matthew 19:26

The divorce debate follows this same pattern (see chart):

ACTION	SCRIPTURE
1. Pharisees' Question: "Is it lawful for a man to divorce his wife for any and every reason?"	Matthew 19:3
2. Jesus' Fundamental Challenge to Principle of Divorce: "Haven't you read? ... what God has joined together, let man not separate."	Matthew 19:4 – 6
3. Pharisees' Counterattack: "Why then ... did Moses command ...?"	Matthew 19:7
4. Jesus' Dismissal of Objection: "Moses permitted you to divorce your wives because your hearts were hard.... I tell you that anyone who divorces his wife, except for marital unfaithfulness, and marries another woman commits adultery."	Matthew 19:8 – 9
5. Disciples' Objection: "If this is the situation ..., it is better not to marry."	Matthew 19:10
6. Jesus' Reaffirmation of His Position: "Not everyone can accept this word, but only those to whom it has been given.... The one who can accept this should accept it."	Matthew 19:11 – 12

The most important point to grasp about this pattern is that Jesus does not back down or make concessions to the original questioner or to the disciples when they object to his teaching. Instead, he enlarges on his original point or restates it in a vivid way and challenges his hearers to have the faith to accept his teaching.

It is this context that makes the permissive interpretation of Matthew 19:9 so unlikely. The interpretation that allows divorce and remarriage for *porneia* (sexual immorality) makes Jesus agree with one side in the Pharisaic debate, the Shammaite Pharisees, who allowed divorce and remarriage in a few cases. But the whole thrust of his teaching up to this point has been that divorce is contrary to God's creation purposes (19:4–6). The Pharisees correctly read this as a rejection of their concept of divorce, so they counterattack by quoting Deuteronomy 24:1: "Why then ... did Moses command that a man give his wife a certificate of divorce and send her away?" (19:7).

We should now expect Jesus to reject the Pharisaic view and reaffirm his own teaching. The no-remarriage view fits this perfectly. By only permitting divorce (i.e., separation) for *porneia* and by ruling out remarriage, Jesus shows that his views are quite different from both Pharisaic positions.

This view also explains the disciples' objection in verse 10. Quentin Quesnell notes that "the whole thrust of the passage has been toward building up the greatness and sanctity before God of monogamous marriage, the importance of the bond between spouses, as an expression of the divine will for man from the beginning. Then in verse 10 the disciples reject this picture of life utterly. 'If such is the case of a man with his wife, it is better not to marry.'"[14]

Jesus' response should not be read as a concession to the disciples, as it would be if verses 10–12 were simply a call to celibacy. This is the way many commentators and gospel critics have read it. Such a reading would be totally out of character in Matthew's gospel. Quesnell writes, "The ordinary function of the disciples' speeches in the gospels is to ask questions, to misunderstand or object, or simply to advance the action dramatically. They do not enunciate the Christian ideal for life. Their objections are not accepted and confirmed by the Master, but are refuted, or made the occasion for stronger restatements of the original teaching."[15]

These verses, then, are "a challenging formulation of the state of a man whose wife has been put away (set loose) on account of *porneia*."[16] He may not remarry, so in a sense he is like others who do not marry, who are born eunuchs, and who are made eunuchs by men. Quesnell makes this observation: "Having rebuffed the disciples' attack in characteristic fashion —with a rebuke to them for lack of faith necessary to receive the difficult word—Jesus repeats the call to understanding: He who can grasp it, let him grasp it."[17] Similar calls to faith are found in Matthew 13:9 ("He who has ears, let him hear") and Mark 4:9.

Read this way, Matthew 19:3–12 is coherent and logical, building to a climax in the fashion typical of Jesus' disputes with his opponents. There is no need to suppose different gospels disagree on what Jesus taught about marriage or to suppose that he backed down when challenged by the Pharisees or his disciples. Within the context of Matthew's gospel, let alone the rest of the New Testament and the witness of the early church, a permissive remarriage view is a most improbable interpretation.

The Context within Judaism

I turn now to the context of the life of Jesus and his teaching within the setting of first-century Judaism. I've already discussed this in passing as we looked at the other contexts, and it is discussed more fully in my *Jesus and Divorce*. For those who allow for remarriage after divorce, the argument from the Jewish context is quite simple: All Jews in the first century permitted divorce in certain cases, and a Jewish divorce always entailed the right to remarry. Therefore, any Jewish reader of the New Testament would understand that when divorce was mentioned, it included the right to remarry.[18]

Now no one would dispute that Jews, Greeks, and Romans in the first century assumed that a divorce entitled one to remarry. It is plain, too, that the Old Testament tolerates divorce with the right to remarry, though it also quite clearly does not like it. Many first-century Jews supposed that since God allowed divorce in the Old Testament, he did not object to it or even approved of it. But does this mean that Jesus shared the same thinking? Could he not have taught something different from first-century Jews? For this is basically how the argument goes: When Jesus used the word "divorce" (*apolyein*), he must have been using it in the sense that those contemporary Jews used it.

This seems implausible to me for three reasons. First, Christians have always supposed that at some points Jesus did disagree with contemporary Jews. Why were there so many dispute stories in the Gospels if Jesus taught only what his contemporaries believed?

Second, it is clear that the Pharisees expected him to disagree with them about divorce. As both Matthew and Mark observe, the Pharisees came to test him (Matt. 19:3; Mark 10:2). This was one of several episodes in which Jewish leaders came to him to debate political or theological issues to attempt to make his "heretical" views public (Matt. 16:1; 21:23; 22:15, 23, 34). They were out to prove that he disagreed with their interpretation of the law of the Old Testament. But if the divorce-with-remarriage view is correct, Jesus is just another Pharisee who supported the school of Shammai.[19]

Third, this view rests on a linguistic fallacy. It is a recognized principle of linguistics that the sense of a word exists not in the word alone but also in the utterances in which it is embedded. So it is quite unwarranted to argue that because *apolyein* means "to divorce" (permitting remarriage) in the mouth of the Pharisees, it cannot mean "to separate" (without remarrying) in the mouth of Jesus. It is the context that must decide the nuance in each case. I have already stated my reasons for believing that when Jesus talks of *apolyein*, he is talking merely of separation without the right to remarry. This is the only sense that fits the context.[20]

But there is a final consideration. Even permissive interpreters who hold that Jesus did allow remarriage after divorce for *porneia* admit that, according to Jesus, *apolyein* did not always allow remarriage after divorce.[21] They essentially understand Matthew 19:9 to cover two situations: (1) whoever divorces his wife in a non-*porneia* case and marries another commits adultery; (2) whoever divorces his wife in the case of *porneia* and marries another does not commit adultery.

In the second case, the divorce is full and proper because remarriage does not count as adultery. However, in the first case, not even the husband is free to remarry without committing adultery. In other words, the legal form of divorce does not give the right to remarry. So we ought to render the first case (1) whoever separates from his wife and marries another commits adultery. In other words, *apolyein* here does not mean "divorce with the right to remarry" but only "separation." So here Jesus is using *apolyein* in a different sense from his Jewish opponents. At most, permissive interpreters can argue that sometimes Jesus uses *apolyein* to mean "divorce," but sometimes he means only "separate." They cannot argue that *apolyein* *always* means "divorce with the right to remarry."[22]

Finally, if we admit that Jesus is using *apolyein* in a different sense from the Pharisees, is this not to accuse him (or Matthew) of being obscure? Not at all. It is a great example of Jesus' verbal dexterity. It demonstrates his command of language and the debate process. No one can read the Gospels without being amazed at his vivid and striking use of language. He takes up old terms and gives them new meanings. Dupont notes that in another dispute with the Pharisees about purity, Jesus does just the same sort of thing.[23] The Pharisees followed the Old Testament law, which said that what you ate and touched made you unclean, but Jesus said, "It is not what goes into the mouth that defiles a person, but what comes out of the mouth" (Matt 15:11 ESV). Jesus takes familiar Jewish terminology and fills it with new meaning; he does the same when discussing divorce.

My brother David has observed that this type of quip or pun is entirely characteristic of Jesus' teaching.[24] Talking with Nicodemus, Jesus reinterpreted what being "born again" means; with the woman of Samaria the meaning of "living water"; and with the Pharisees the meaning of "blindness" (John 3:3–7; 4:10–14; 9:38–41). The Synoptic Gospels often show Jesus picking up a term used by someone else and giving it a different meaning. For example, "Someone told [Jesus], 'Your mother and brothers are standing outside, wanting to see you.' He replied, 'My mother and brothers are those who hear God's word and put it into practice'" (Luke 8:20–21; cf. Matt. 12:46–50; Mark 3:32–35). At his trial and while he hung on the cross, he was accused of having said, "I am able to destroy the temple of God and rebuild it in three days" (Matt. 26:61; cf. 27:40; Mark 14:58; 15:29). John 2:21 explains what Jesus meant: "the temple he had spoken of was his body." When children were brought to Jesus, he spoke first of children and then of "little ones." It would be easy to equate the two, but a more careful reading shows that "little ones" are not necessarily youngsters but humble believers (Matt. 18:5–6; Mark 9:42). Finally, one could argue that Jesus enjoyed this sort of quip from an early age! Having at last found him in the temple, Mary scolded, "Your father and I have been anxiously searching for you." He replied, "Didn't you know I had to be in my Father's house?" (Luke 2:48–49). In light of these examples, it could be argued that it would be strange if Jesus had not used *apolyein* in a different sense from his opponents.

Thus, all these New Testament contexts point in the same direction, namely, that separation was allowed for *porneia*, i.e., in situations where Jewish and Roman law required divorce for sexual immorality, but remarriage was never approved. No one, not even ardent defenders of the permissive view, contests that the early church held this view. But if one holds that the permissive view is the original sense of Jesus' teaching, it becomes a great mystery as to how the early church came to hold the view that remarriage after divorce is wrong. On this improbable scenario, second-century Christians would have had both the apostolic tradition and non-Christian practice endorsing the right to remarry. What on earth could have persuaded the whole church to adopt the strict discipline of no remarriage after divorce? This was no minor adjustment to doctrine or ethics. It potentially affected the lifestyle of every member of the church and every potential convert. It does not seem likely that it could be based simply on the ignorance of Gentiles who were reading the Gospels, who did not know the Jewish customs about divorce entailing the right to remarry, for, in fact, there was plenty of interaction between Jews and Christians in the early centuries.[25]

Similar principles prevailed elsewhere in the Roman Empire. Divorce allowed people to remarry. So why should second-century Christians suddenly have started to read the Gospels in a way that was contrary both to contemporary custom and the traditions of Jesus that they had inherited from the apostolic age? I find this scenario historically implausible. I believe that only our Lord could have persuaded his followers to make this immense change in marriage discipline and thus break with both Jewish and classical tradition.

APPLYING NEW TESTAMENT TEACHING TODAY

I am sure what I have written will shock and dismay many readers. You may say to yourself, "I never realized it was wrong for me to remarry or to have encouraged someone else to remarry." It is most important to realize that if this is your situation, God *will* forgive you. An old hymn puts it beautifully.

There's a wideness in God's mercy
Like the wideness of the sea;
There's a kindness in his justice
Which is more than liberty.

There is no place where earth's sorrows
Are more felt than up in heaven;
There is no place where earth's failings
Have such kindly judgment given.

The prophets picture God as having experienced divorce and all the pain associated with it, so he certainly understands your situation if that is what you or your friends are going through. Furthermore, it is obvious that those who have never been taught that divorce and remarriage are wrong are less to blame than those who have been taught that Jesus condemned it. We all sin unknowingly at times, which is why Jesus taught us to pray not only for daily bread but also for forgiveness of our sins. We need forgiveness each day just as much as we need daily bread.

So my first point is that if my conclusions have convicted you, do not despair, but turn to our great high priest who is able to sympathize with our weaknesses "so that we may receive mercy and find grace to help us in our time of need" (Heb. 4:16).

But can we go further? Everyone can see that our society is suffering terribly as the result of marital instability. A hundred years ago, divorce was very rare. Of course, that is not to say that all marriages were happy or that no one committed adultery, but such an atmosphere must have, on balance, made for much greater psychological stability and social cohesiveness than we see today with our rampant individualism.

The situation is so bad that it's difficult to know what to do. If pastors speak up on this subject, they will offend many in their congregations. If politicians propose legislation that would favor traditional families, they will lose the votes of single parents and like-minded people. As Amos said, "The prudent man keeps quiet in such times, for the times are evil" (5:13). Nevertheless, the Old Testament prophets, as well as Jesus and Paul, were willing to speak out, despite the unpopularity it caused. And I think the modern church should do the same.

Action Priority: Education

So how *should* we act? The first priority is, of course, education. We cannot change the attitudes and practices of people unless they are aware of Christ's standards. To ban second marriages in a church that has long permitted them is to court disaster and will achieve very little, unless it is done with the broad consent of its membership. So at every level of church life, from the seminary to the home, our Lord's teaching about marriage must be passed on. In the local church, marriage should be a subject that is discussed at every level. Particularly important will be the teaching given to teenagers in youth groups and to couples in marriage preparation classes. Every engaged couple should have several sessions that deal with both the theology of marriage and practical aspects of married life. People today often spend more time learning how to drive than how to be married.

Ministers should also preach about marriage. Obviously they must emphasize the positive value of marriage as it is portrayed in the Bible, but they must not shy away from the difficult issues of divorce, remarriage, and singleness. To do so will require great sensitivity, since most congregations contain both divorced and remarried people. In his book *Divorce and Remarriage*, Andrew Cornes says that before he preached a series of sermons on these topics, he arranged five meetings with a group of divorced and remarried members of his congregation in which he explained what he wanted to say in his sermons, listened to their comments, and heard their life stories. He observed that "this was of the utmost benefit to me.... As a series, it has provoked more discussion and thought than any other in living memory."[26]

Action Priority: Caring

The second priority of the church is caring. It is the Christian's duty to bear one another's burdens, not to pass by on the other side. Individual church members should be alert to their friends' needs. If someone senses that a couple is having problems, they should encourage them to sort it out. This must be done with great sensitivity, or it will be rejected as interference. But probably more of us suffer from an excess of timidity than the opposite fault. We live in an age that tells us we are all individuals and everyone must be allowed to do their own thing, no matter how bad it might be for them. So we are reluctant to get involved in other people's affairs. But Scripture teaches us that we are all part of the body of Christ, and that we have a duty to care for each other (1 Cor. 12:24–26).

This mutual concern must especially be extended to those who have been divorced, who suffer tremendous pain and guilt and encounter many practical difficulties. They need reassurance that no matter what they have done in the past, God cares for them—and he will forgive them if they seek it. Friends must be ready to listen and sympathize and give the support that the divorced person needs. It can be a tricky path to pursue, because we need to support the person in a nonjudgmental manner without giving the impression that it was a good thing to terminate the marriage. In supportive counseling, it is necessary to bear witness gently and compassionately to God's standards, as well as to the fullness of his love and forgiveness.

More practically, the loneliness of the divorced person needs to be recognized and catered to. So many social functions cater to couples that singles often feel left out, and this is even more painful if one has known the joys of marriage. Old Testament law is particularly concerned with the needs of widows and orphans. The widespread breakdown of marriage has sadly increased the scope of this category, and we need to be especially aware of the needs of single persons for friendship. More than that, we need to value the contribution that single people make to church and society. Their freedom from family commitments should be an asset to both the church and the community (Matt. 19:12; 1 Cor. 7:32–33).

It is not simply the duty of individual Christians to care for the divorced and the separated, but the church community should support them too. Larger churches may have pastors who have responsibility to minister to families. There should be opportunities in private and public worship for divorced people and others to hear God's promises of forgiveness. Cornes writes, "I cannot stress enough that one of the greatest needs of the divorcée is to deal with his or her guilt. He often finds it very hard to forgive himself or to feel forgiven by God."[27]

Action Priority: Worship and Church Discipline

I think it would also be helpful to consider the style of our worship. In my experience, evangelical worship tends to be almost entirely praise oriented. But if one looks at the psalms, the most common category is laments, psalms in which the worshiper pours out his complaint to God and prays for help and healing. In our congregations, there are many who come to worship bearing great pain in their souls, and they need the opportunity to express their woes to God. If the way is not clear for them to do so, they will feel even more excluded and cut off from their fellow worshipers and from God.

Another aspect of caring is church discipline. It is not sufficient simply to teach Jesus' marriage principles and to support those who fail. It is necessary to uphold those principles when people disregard them. In the present divided state of Protestantism, this is well-nigh impossible, because if Church A will not remarry you, Church B just down the road will. In two denominations in the United Kingdom—the Methodist Church and United Reformed Church—half the weddings involve people who have been divorced. The reason? Because the Church of England and Roman Catholics have traditionally been unwilling to remarry people. Nevertheless, the early church usually excommunicated for long periods members who remarried after divorce, indeed, sometimes for the rest of their lives. Origen tells us that some bishops in Egypt allowed remarriage "to avoid worse evils," although they knew doing so was contrary to Jesus' teaching. So throughout church history, discipline in this area has been a very messy business. But unless principles are enforced, we may as well give up the attempt to teach the permanency of marriage.

Though some people may leave the church if marriage discipline is enforced, others may leave if it is not. Cornes mentions the case of a man who left his wife and married someone else from the church. This remarried couple then was promoted to an office in the church, where the deserted wife was still worshiping. Her outrage at the church's stance can well be imagined. But having said that churches must uphold Jesus' principles by both their practice and their teaching, I am very reluctant to lay down guidelines. The issue of just how strict the discipline should be, it seems to me, should depend on where a church is at the moment. We should be aware of what Jesus teaches and seek to move our church in that direction, but we cannot expect changes of attitude or practice overnight.

In this matter, we must distinguish between tolerance and approval. The Old Testament clearly tolerates divorce and remarriage, but never, I think, approves of it. As Jesus said, "Moses permitted you to divorce your wives because your hearts were hard. But it was not this way from the beginning"

(Matt. 19:8). Following Jesus' teaching, the New Testament church took a much tougher stance. Though they sometimes tolerated divorce for *porneia* (Matt. 5:32) or desertion (1 Cor. 7:15), they never tolerated, let alone approved of, remarriage after divorce. Regrettably, many modern churches have slipped back into Old Testament attitudes. Indeed, some would seem to be even more liberal than the Old Testament by actually approving of, not simply tolerating, divorce and remarriage. Somehow we have to move our churches and our society to accept the standards Jesus insisted on. It will be a very difficult and slow process. I fear it will take decades, not years. But with persistence and God's help, the situation may change.

Let's imagine a church that is moving from its currently permissive stance toward divorce and remarriage to a more restrictive stance. Change would start by teaching Jesus' principles at all levels of church life. The care of divorced people and other singles would be just as important to stress as the restriction on remarriage. When Jesus' teachings come to be widely understood, it may be that the congregation will become restive about remarrying divorced persons in church; and with the consent of the leaders in the church, the pastor may feel empowered to decline future requests for remarriage. Subsequently, the issue of remarried church officers may come up, and in the course of time it may be thought improper to appoint them to positions of leadership in the church. First Timothy 3:2, 12 insist that overseers and deacons in the church must be married only once. At some stage in the process, it may seem right to exclude from fellowship those whom the Anglican Book of Common Prayer calls "open and notorious evil livers."

All these changes would have to be implemented gradually and with great discretion. If a permissive congregation is pushed too hard, it will resist and probably throw out its pastor and appoint someone more suited to their taste. Then nothing will have been achieved. The most effective leaders are those who stay close to their people.

Action Priority: Politics

A final area of concern is that of politics. The present breakdown in marriage is costing society dearly. Children do poorly in school. There is delinquency among young people and depression among the old. Social services are overstretched in responding to spousal and child abuse. Vast sums are spent on supporting single-parent families.[28] In the United Kingdom, a policy of so-called equality means that in many respects people are better-off financially to cohabit than to marry. Those who divorce get various benefits denied to married couples. This is one of the pressures that discourages marriage today.

So we need financial experts and media gurus who will point out these problems to our political leaders, and thus help get our laws changed in ways that will support marriage. We need divorce lawyers who do not see it as their first and only duty to facilitate their clients' cases as quickly as possible but who try to explore whether there may be a chance to save the marriage first. We need sex education programs in schools that do not just teach about sexual techniques and condoms but encourage abstinence before marriage and lifelong fidelity within marriage. We need restrictions on the media, not simply to prevent pornography, but to encourage lifestyles that are dedicated to the good of the other and not merely to self-gratification. We must work for a world where Christ's standards are honored, not only in the hearts of the faithful, but in our laws and in the institutions that regulate our lives.

A RESPONSE TO GORDON J. WENHAM

William A. Heth

Gordon Wenham's position that Christians should not remarry after divorce for whatever reason is the view that I championed in everything I published between 1982 and 1997. In the early 1980s, we coauthored a book that set forth a modified version of the early church's no-remarriage understanding of Jesus' teaching. *Jesus and Divorce* first appeared in the United Kingdom in 1984 and in the USA in 1985, and we collaborated on an updated version in 1997. I will be ever grateful for the influence Gordon Wenham has had on my life and count him as my mentor and a dear friend.

As I will state in the conclusion to my chapter, some very good arguments can be made for a no-remarriage view. Gordon has summarized most of these in his chapter. This view, as difficult as it is to apply, would be certain if we could be sure of two major points: (1) that Jesus' teachings, especially his statement that "anyone who marries the divorced woman commits adultery" (Matt. 5:32b; cf. Luke 16:18b), are aimed directly at countering the freedom for remarriage expressed in the Jewish bill of divorce; and (2) that Paul's statement in 1 Corinthians 7:15 ("is not bound") does *not* imply freedom for remarriage.

REASONS MY VIEW CHANGED

Over time, I began to doubt the certainty of these points and thus launched out in a new direction. Many of the reasons for doing so still remain after reading Gordon's chapter. I concluded that (1) I misconstrued the significance of marriage as a "kinship" relationship; (2) I was mistaken about the nature and permanence of biblical marriage covenants; (3) I downplayed the seriousness with which God views the sin of adultery; (4) I did not fully appreciate the significance of the cultural *and biblical* recognition of the differences between valid and invalid divorces; and (5) I did not give enough consideration to Jewish interpretive traditions and cultural assumptions that first-century readers brought to their reading of the New Testament.

Two additional personal observations led me to reconstruct my interpretive framework. First, I could not come up with a satisfactory biblical answer for the practical dilemmas caused by a blanket no-remarriage conclusion. Upon hearing about my no-remarriage position, a fellow seminary student blurted out, "Do you mean to tell me that my friend, whose wife left him and his four kids for a lesbian, has to remain single for the rest of his life?" To "suffer for what is right" (1 Pet. 3:14) may well cover such cases, given the assumption that marriage is indissoluble. However, I struggled with why Jesus would impose such remarriage restrictions on an offended innocent party.

A second personal concern bothered me. For fifteen years, I tried to make the best case possible for a no-remarriage understanding of the New Testament teaching, yet I was not able to persuade other New Testament scholars whom I greatly respected. I knew my own intellectual limitations well enough not to presume that I *must* be right.

COULD ALL OF THE EARLY CHRISTIAN WRITERS HAVE MISUNDERSTOOD?

The four points of Gordon's argument for a no-remarriage understanding of Jesus' teaching are coherent and tightly interconnected. The question he asks — "Could all of the early Christian writers have misunderstood the gospel divorce texts?" — leads me to ask this question: "If Jesus *had* permitted remarriage, what motivated the church fathers to take a more stringent stand?" The unanimity of the early church's no-remarriage teaching has to be reckoned with.

Readers can work with two hypotheses: (1) Gordon is right, and these early writers were faithfully passing on what Jesus taught; or (2) the church fathers restricted Jesus' prohibition in line with a growing asceticism in the early church. I find the latter more probable. This asceticism was visible in embryonic form already in the New Testament (cf. 1 Cor. 7:1, 28, 36; 1 Tim. 4:3; Col. 2:21), and it eventually led to the requirement that ministers in the Roman Catholic Church be celibate. The extent to which this asceticism manifested itself is evident in those writers who disallowed second marriages *even after the death of a spouse* (Athenagoras, Tertullian, Clement of Alexandria), contrary to the clear teaching of the apostle Paul (1 Cor. 7:39). Athenagoras (ca. AD 177) went so far as to refer to marriage after a spouse's death as a veiled form of adultery! Most of these writers also took a very dim view of sexual relations within marriage, much like the ascetics Paul confronted in Corinth (1 Cor. 7:1b). In effect, most church fathers said, "Marital relations are only for begetting children, and even then you'd better not enjoy it!" This was hardly the teaching of Paul (1 Cor. 7:2–6; 1 Tim. 4:4).

HOW GORDON AND I AGREE AND DIFFER

Gordon and I agree that Jesus *did* have a major conflict with the Jews of his day. We differ on whether Jesus was *totally* restrictive on remarriage after any divorce (Wenham) or *almost totally* restrictive (Heth). We agree that Jesus radically redefined the permanence of marriage in view of God's creation design. He firmly opposed the dominant Hillelite "no fault" divorce practices; but the exception clause in Matthew points to some type of agreement with the minority view of Shammai. As far as the debated Deuteronomy 24:1 ground is concerned, Jesus recognized adultery as constituting a valid or legitimate ground for divorce. Adultery *is* a major violation of the marriage covenant (cf. 1 Thess. 4:6). But unlike Shammai, Jesus did not require, but probably *permitted*, divorce and remarriage. Jesus' teachings, rather, stressed marriage's permanence and the need for the forgiveness and repentance that could keep a marriage intact.

So *if* Jesus' divorce sayings were powerful prophetic statements (Mark and Luke) intended to do away with all the Hillelite abuses, *and if* they were not intended to be taken as exceptionless absolutes (Matt. 5:32; 19:9; 1 Cor 7:15), then the disciples' exasperation with Jesus' teaching in Matthew 19:10 is readily explained on the view that Jesus restricted valid grounds for divorce and remarriage to those that took place because of unrepentant sexual immorality. I agree that Jesus does not back off from driving home the idea of lifelong permanence of marriage in the face of the disciples' objection in Matthew 19:10. Matthew 19:11–12 can even be understood as Jesus' assurance that divine enablement to remain single is given to those who divorce or have been divorced for *reasons other than unchastity* (v. 9). Thus, interpreting Matthew 19 to allow remarriage after a legitimate divorce does not make Jesus contradict himself.

I agree with Gordon that explicit permission to remarry is far from Jesus' mind when he speaks out against divorce and remarriage. I agree that the exception clause in Matthew 5:32 may well indicate only that "should a wife have already committed adultery, her husband can hardly be said to have made her commit adultery." When readers encounter "exceptions" in New Testament divorce texts like Matthew 19:9 ("except for marital unfaithfulness") and 1 Corinthians 7:15 ("A believing man or woman is not bound in such circumstances"), there are really only two ways to interpret them. These exceptional situations either permit (1) divorce *but not* remarriage, or (2) divorce *and* remarriage. I would contend that the most natural assumption first-century readers would bring to these texts is that a legitimate ground for divorce is specified, and a valid divorce left permission for remarriage. Given the readers' assumptions, neither Jesus nor Paul would have had to specify that remarriage is permitted. But *a prohibition of remarriage* where valid grounds for divorce *are specified* in that first-century culture would require greater clarification by the biblical writers.

The strongest argument I find for believing that Jesus did not want his disciples to remarry is that in both Testaments marriage is a picture of the relationship between God and Israel and between Christ and the church. To this I would add that Paul exhorts believers to follow his example as he imitates Christ (1 Cor. 4:16; 11:1), and Jesus calls his disciples to become the kind of people who share the characteristics of God himself (Matt. 5:44–48; cf. Eph. 4:1–2). In the Old Testament, God lovingly pursued unrepentant Israel and seemingly refused to cast her off. If believers are to be imitators of Christ and God, they would seemingly never give up on the hope of restoring a relationship, no matter what has arisen to destroy it. But as I note in my chapter, fallen humanity this side of a renewed heaven and earth is not quite parallel in the comparison to either Christ or God.

I resonate with so much of what Gordon writes in the final application section of his chapter. As one of my pastor friends recently told me, "Most, if not all, of the divorce and potential remarriage cases do not seem to come close to the mostly restrictive view that you hold, let alone the totally restrictive view that others hold. Even if they do, I have yet to see one work hard to reconcile. We're a 'throwaway marriage' culture, and it is so terribly sad." Everything Gordon writes in his concluding section would help turn around this state of affairs in the church.

A RESPONSE TO GORDON J. WENHAM

Craig S. Keener

I appreciate the points of agreement that Gordon rightly articulates in his opening section. Certainly, exceptions must remain exceptional and not the focus, or some will exploit as loopholes for sin our arguments originally meant to defend the innocent or to extend mercy.

Yet, on the practical, pastoral level, Gordon's universal prohibition of remarriage has implications more serious than he himself would probably acknowledge. We must reckon with the demands of what his own argument should, if followed consistently, imply. If remarriage is always and literally adulterous, it is so because it is a new union while the former union remains in effect in God's sight. Although Gordon may not wish to draw this conclusion in practice, this view logically entails that the marriage, not the wedding, must be adulterous. If this were the case, it would hardly be sufficient to merely offer forgiveness to those who are sorry, as Gordon seems ready to do. If remarriages are adulterous, we should break up the adulterous unions; to do less is to tolerate the intolerable, namely, continuing adultery. While such a solution may appear tenable in the case of, say, a recent marriage that culminates an affair, its pastoral implications are daunting for those remarried years earlier and now raising children.

EVALUATING GORDON'S ARGUMENTS

The truth of a view cannot be determined simply by how painful its demands are, however, so I now address Gordon's supporting arguments. His strongest argument is actually not biblical (see the discussion below) but is his argument from early church history. I respect the church fathers and learn from their wisdom wherever possible, but this is one of the cases where an appeal to them is vulnerable. The no-remarriage view is first attested in the fourth mandate (1:6) of the *Shepherd of Hermas*, a work that heavily influenced later interpretations. Hermas reflects a rising current of asceticism that goes beyond the apostolic witness; he prefers celibate singleness after widowhood and introduces the notions of penance and only one permissible repentance.[1] Many of the writers on which Gordon depends also endorsed priestly celibacy; Augustine sent away his concubine, the mother of his son, and broke an engagement to follow this ideal. Such developments reflect the widespread rise of sexual asceticism in late antiquity; the church fathers, just like the biblical writers, addressed cultural settings often different from our own.

The Greek fathers (unlike some Western writers like Augustine) did know Greek, but only a few of the Fathers were very familiar with the Jewish context of Jesus and Paul. While Jerome and Hippolytus were such exceptions, the philosopher Justin, whom Gordon cites, is less so (though raised as a Gentile in Samaria, he claims no knowledge of Judaism before his adulthood). Although Justin shows acquaintance with many Jewish traditions (e.g., details about the scapegoat; polygamy; the hidden Messiah; "Man" as a divine title), he often misunderstands or misrepresents Judaism (e.g., lack of law-keeping before Moses; the Messiah's divinity or suffering; application of Psalm 110 to Hezekiah [rather than to Abraham]). Contrary to Gordon's implication, even Justin's Trypho does not know Hebrew and generally handles Scripture in a nonrabbinic way (though this is not too surprising for a second-century Diaspora Jew).[2] Gordon's claim that Akiba was a convert from Christianity is simply false. Few today would endorse some ideas, including the anti-Judaism, of some of the Fathers, borrowed from common Gentile stereotypes of Judaism. Yet even the tradition-respecting Byzantine church did not, in fact, prevent all remarriages.

When the Reformers revisited the biblical texts in question, respectful of but no longer dependent on intervening centuries of tradition, most concluded in favor of remarriage in the case of divorce for adultery. Characterizing this view as "the permissive Erasmian view" rhetorically biases the case; why not call it the "Reformation view" or call its alternative the "legalistic" view?

As to whether there are exceptions or not, exceptions are explicitly stated. The question is not, against Gordon here, making Jesus contradict himself—exceptions by definition qualify general rules; the real question is whether we should read, as Bill Heth and I do, the smaller number of texts (that merely assume exceptions) in light of the larger number (that state them); or, as some no-remarriage proponents do, read the larger number of texts in light of the smaller number. That is, should we explain Jesus' generalized and terse statements as general principle and hyperbole (demonstrably common in his teaching), or as exceptionless rules that make nonsense of the normal meaning of the exceptions?

But do the exceptions apply to divorce, or to remarriage? The exception clause is appended to divorce rather than to remarriage because it is the *validity* of the divorce that establishes the basis for acceptable remarriage. If the text allows a divorce as valid, it also allows the remarriage to be valid. A remarriage is "adulterous" by definition if—and only if—the divorce was invalid (Matthew refers only to remarriage, *not* to divorce itself this way, because "adultery" by definition involves a different union).

Valid divorce, by ancient definition, conferred the right to remarry, as Gordon grants. That Jesus could redefine "divorce" if he wished to do so, as Gordon suggests, is not in question; but that he could do so hardly proves that he did do so. In fact, unless we wish to throw all of Scripture into lexical confusion, the burden of proof must remain on those who argue for novel word meanings (beyond their otherwise-attested semantic range), and I do not believe that such proof has been offered. Without compelling evidence, we cannot make the exception clause mean something other than what it meant in ancient sources. To counter by saying that we argue that Jesus allowed divorce simply because his contemporaries did so, or to reduce our entire argument to that claim, caricatures our argument. (For example, I did argue that Jesus spoke more radically than the school of Shammai, though he agreed with their exception.)[3]

Gordon reads Jesus' invitation to singleness in Matthew 19:11–12 as a reaffirmation of 19:9 (apparently regardless of that verse's exception), but this is possible only by dramatically reinterpreting the intervening verse. The disciples in verse 10 fear not remarriage but marrying to begin with, if such marriage cannot include an escape clause. (Many ancient marriage contracts included arrangements in case of divorce.) Jesus answers their radical solution (singleness) with another radical statement addressing not specifically divorced people but anyone with the gift of singleness (cf. 1 Cor. 7:7–9); the general context is not only divorce but family (cf. Matt. 19:13–15). Gordon compares 13:9 as a summons to all; but its context is quite different (and Matthew also includes some statements to limited groups; e.g., 13:52; 16:17–18, 28).[4] Although Gordon cites some commentators who support his position, most Matthew commentators (of whom I am one) do not find this line of argument persuasive.

Paul does, as Gordon notes, quote Jesus' prohibition of divorce and remarriage in 1 Corinthians 7:10–11; but then Paul immediately qualifies this prohibition for a special situation in 7:12–15—something Paul can do precisely and only because he takes Jesus' words as a general statement that can be qualified. (If the Fathers knew Greek better than we do, Paul knew Jesus' context better than the Fathers did.) Gordon quotes Gordon Fee in support; but as the latter himself reminded me recently, his commentary denies only that the text speaks to the issue, yet he points readers to the larger context of Scripture and argues that remarriages can be redemptive.[5]

RESPONDING TO GORDON'S PRACTICAL IMPLICATIONS

Regarding the pastoral implications Gordon draws, I appreciate his sensitivity to the loneliness of those who face divorce and who, on his view, cannot find solace in another marriage. I also concur with his insistence on church discipline (especially in the sort of example he mentions); if divorce is a justice issue that requires support for an aggrieved party (where one exists), it also demands discipline for the party (or parties) who have acted unjustly.

I further recognize that other cultures are appalled by Western family values, though I would suggest that most of those cultures are more appalled by sexual immorality than by the thought of divorcing a sexually immoral partner. Rampant divorce is indeed appalling, but does remarriage fall into the same category? May it not often reduce the problems Gordon associates with single-parent households? Legal no-fault divorce is likely part of the problem; but I would argue that remarriage for a party wronged by a partner's persistent adultery, abandonment, or abuse is not part of the problem. The "sexual revolution" has increased all these problems, as it has increased divorce, but we ought not to confuse cause with effect.

Chapter 1: No Remarriage after Divorce

1. See Meic Pearse, *Why the Rest Hate the West* (London: SPCK, 2003).

2. The full arguments for this view are set out in W. A. Heth and G. J. Wenham, *Jesus and Divorce* (3rd ed.; Carlisle: Paternoster, 2002). See also G. J. Wenham, "Does the NT approve remarriage after divorce?" *Southern Baptist Journal of Theology* 6 (2002): 30–45.

3. The definitive discussion of what the early church believed about divorce and remarriage is found in Henri Crouzel, *L'Église primitive face au divorce* (Paris: Beauchesne, 1971). The material that follows is drawn primarily from this important work.

4. See Crouzel, *L'Église primitive*, 360.

5. Gordon D. Fee, *The First Epistle to the Corinthians* (NICNT; Grand Rapids: Eerdmans, 1987), 296.

6. See G. J. Wenham, "Gospel Definitions of Adultery and Women's Rights," *ExpTim* 95 (1984): 330–32.

7. The case of Herodias is often cited, but, as J. Dupont (*Mariage et divorce dans l'évangile* [Bruges: Desclée de Brouwer, 1959], 63) observes, she just abandoned her husband. It could be that Jesus is just aware of what was possible under Greek and Roman law (so C. E. B. Cranfield, *The Gospel according to St Mark* [Cambridge: Cambridge Univ. Press, 1963], 322).

8. For a discussion of the meaning of the Greek word *porneia*, see Heth and Wenham, *Jesus and Divorce*, 183–84. *Porneia* covers a wide range of sexual sins condemned in the OT law.

9. So Raymond F. Collins, *Divorce in the New Testament* (GNS 38; Collegeville, Minn.: Liturgical Press, 1992), 167.

10. Dupont (*Mariage et divorce*, 131–32) sets out the illogicality most lucidly: "If, according to v.32a, remarriage is allowed after divorce for *porneia* but in no other situation, v.32b has absurd consequences. It must be paraphrased 'Whoever marries a divorced woman is adulterous if this woman has not behaved culpably towards the husband who divorced her. But he is not adulterous if this woman has been divorced for misbehaving.' Such conclusions are manifestly absurd." Dupont points out that this difficulty is reduced if the innocent husband has the right to remarry but not his guilty wife. But if she is not allowed to remarry, it implies she is still bound to her husband, and he to her. Thus when he remarries, he is effectively taking a second wife and is thus, at least in the eyes of God, a polygamist.

11. See G. J. Wenham, "Matthew and Divorce: An Old Crux Revisited," *JSNT* 22 (1984): 95–107; Wenham, "The Syntax of Matthew 19:9," *JSNT* 28 (1986): 17–23.

12. H. D. Betz, *The Sermon on the Mount* (Minneapolis: Fortress, 1995), 257.

13. Other examples in Matthew include 15:1–20; 20:20–28. Briefer examples of the pattern include 9:10–17; 12:10–13; 19:13–15; 21:23–27.

14. Q. Quesnell, "'Made Themselves Eunuchs for the Kingdom of Heaven' (Mt. 19:12)," *CBQ* 30 (1968): 342.

15. Ibid., 343.

16. Ibid., 346.

17. Ibid., 347.

18. C. S. Keener (… *And Marries Another* [Peabody, Mass.: Hendrickson, 1991], 44) writes, "A valid divorce by standard ancient definition implied the right to remarry…. No ancient Jewish reader would have read Matthew otherwise." The same insistence that Jewish convictions about divorce must determine the interpretation of the New Testament texts is at the heart of David Instone-Brewer's arguments in *Divorce and Remarriage in the 1st and 21st Century* (Cambridge: Grove, 2001) and *Divorce and Remarriage in the Bible: The Social and Literary Context* (Grand Rapids: Eerdmans, 2002).

19. M. D. Goulder notes, "The radical Jesus disappears in qualifying phrases, and emerges as a rabbi of the school of Shammai" (quoted in Collins, *Divorce in the New Testament*, 185).

20. The linguistic situation is even more complicated than this. Clearly Jesus and the Pharisees were debating not in Greek but in Aramaic or possibly Hebrew. So they probably used the term *šālaḥ*, not *apolyō*. What is important to notice is that by themselves these terms are quite general; *šālaḥ* means to send, and *apolyō* to loose, or undo. The precise sense of "divorce" or "separate" is given by the context in which the word is embedded. Compare the English word *wash*. We can picture washing one's face, a car, a dish, or whatever. In each case, quite different actions are involved, and it would be wrong to imagine that a person washes his face in the same way as he washes a car. It is the context of car washing that determines exactly what washing involves in this case.

21. See, e.g., John Murray (*Divorce* [Philadelphia: Presbyterian & Reformed, 1976], 25), who writes, "It follows from what has been said that the man who divorces his wife (except for the cause of fornication) is not thereby at liberty to remarry any more than the divorced wife. If the woman commits adultery by remarriage, this is so because she is still in reality the wife of the divorcing husband. And if so, the divorcing husband is still in reality the husband of the divorced woman and consequently may not marry another."

22. One may well argue that it is awkward, to say the least, to have Jesus using *apolyein* in two different senses simultaneously, and that this is another argument against the permissive interpretation; the early church view is free from this problem, for, in that view, when Jesus uses the word *apolyein*, it always means "separate from." But this is not my main point. I want to stress that permissive interpreters must admit that Jesus is using *apolyein* in a different sense from his Jewish opponents. Because permissive interpreters do allow that Jesus taught that divorce in non-*porneia* cases is adulterous, they are saying that this is not real divorce but merely separation.

23. See Dupont, *Mariage et divorce*, 145–47.

24. In personal conversation.

25. This is David Instone-Brewer's argument, namely, that Christians were cut off from Jews after the first century and were ignorant of Jewish practices. This is nonsense. Justin Martyr's dialogue with Trypho is a debate between a rabbi and a Christian. Akiba, the second-century rabbi, was a

convert from Christianity. J. N. D. Kelly (*Early Christian Doctrines* [San Francisco: HarperSanFrancisco, 1978], 17–22) notes the enduring influence of Jewish thinking on second-century Christology. Alexandria, home of Clement and Origen, was full of Jews. When Origen moved to Caesarea in the third century, he held public debates with local rabbis. The Antiochene school's methods of exegesis are often said to owe much to Jewish approaches. Chrysostom was well aware of Jewish thinking and warned his people not to convert. Jerome learned Hebrew from the Jews so that he could translate the OT from Hebrew. See also Robert M. Grant, *A Short History of the Interpretation of the Bible* (2d ed.; Philadelphia: Fortress, 1984), and C. A. Evans and J. A. Sanders, *The Function of Scripture in Early Jewish and Christian Tradition* (Sheffield: Sheffield Academic Press, 1998).

26. Andrew Cornes, *Divorce and Remarriage* (London: Hodder & Stoughton, 1993), 336–37.

27. Ibid., 381.

28. A recent British report (January 2005) estimated that a single mother with two children receives £11,000 ($20,000) a year in welfare benefits, whereas a married couple with two children on average earnings pays £5,000 ($9,000) in taxes!

Chapter 1: A Response to Gordon J. Wenham (Craig S. Keener)

1. See my "Marriage, Divorce and Adultery," in *Dictionary of the Later New Testament and Its Developments*, ed. Ralph P. Martin and Peter H. Davids (Downers Grove, Ill.: InterVarsity, 1997), 713–14. In a distortion of Hermas's meaning, some Christians in later centuries postponed baptism until their deathbeds, fearing the consequences of postbaptismal sin.

2. See discussions of Justin, e.g., by L. W. Barnard ("The Old Testament and Judaism in the Writings of Justin Martyr," *VT* 14 [Oct. 1964]: 395–406); B. Z. Bokser ("Justin Martyr and the Jews," *JQR* 64 [1973/74]: 97–122, 204–11); and H. P. Schneider ("Some Reflections on the Dialogue of Justin Martyr with Trypho," *SJTh* 15 [June 1962]: 164–75).

3. Gordon is probably correct in his note that Jesus and the Pharisees were using a scribal language (Aramaic or Hebrew) in their debate (though Greek was well known around Jerusalem). But if God inspired our canonical gospels in Greek, how the inspired authors report Jesus in Greek is part of God's message. What is most important here, however, is that the context is *divorce*; hence both the Semitic and Greek terms should carry their normal sense as used in divorce contexts.

4. Gordon also emphasizes the disciples' propensity to object, though this is far less characteristic of Matthew than Mark, who omits their complaint.

5. Gordon D. Fee, *The First Epistle to the Corinthians* (NICNT; Grand Rapids: Eerdmans, 1987), 306. Fee also wrote these words before I and others had pointed out the relevant parallel in ancient divorce contracts.

REMARRIAGE FOR ADULTERY OR DESERTION

Chapter Two

REMARRIAGE FOR ADULTERY
OR DESERTION

REMARRIAGE FOR ADULTERY
OR DESERTION

William A. Heth

The majority view among evangelicals today is that there are two grounds that would permit divorce and remarriage, namely, marital unfaithfulness and desertion by an unbeliever.[1] Both are violations of marriage as a covenant made between two individuals, with God acting as their witness. Two New Testament statements, one by Jesus and one by Paul, support this view:

- "I tell you that anyone who divorces his wife, except for marital unfaithfulness, and marries another woman commits adultery" (Matt. 19:9; cf. 5:32).
- "But if the unbeliever leaves, let him do so. A believing man or woman is not bound in such circumstances; God has called us to live in peace" (1 Cor. 7:15).

For many years I defended the minority view that Jesus and Paul may well have permitted marital separation or legal divorce but that they did not thereby sanction remarriage.[2] I now believe I was mistaken and would like to explain in this chapter the most important reasons why I believe the Scriptures permit divorce and remarriage in the event of a spouse's unrepentant sexual immorality and of desertion by an unbeliever.[3]

MARRIAGE IS A COVENANT, BUT NOT AN UNBREAKABLE ONE (GENESIS 2:24)

Naturally, our attitude toward divorce and remarriage will be determined by our convictions about the nature of the marriage relationship itself. This is why we need to begin with a clear understanding of the Old Testament passage that Jesus cited as the basis for what he taught.

When questioned by the Pharisees concerning his views on the permissibility of divorce "for any and every reason" (Matt. 19:3; cf. Mark 10:2), Jesus cited two texts from Genesis 1 and 2:

> "Haven't you read," he replied, "that at the beginning the Creator 'made them male and female' [Gen. 1:27], and said, 'For this reason a man will leave his father and mother and be united to his wife, and the two will become one flesh' [Gen. 2:24]?"
>
> Matthew 19:4–5

So what can be gleaned from Genesis 2:24 about the nature and permanence of the marriage relationship?

Covenant Language: "Leave and Cleave"

When we read "Therefore shall a man *leave* ... and shall *cleave*" (KJV), we are reading the language of biblical covenants. The term "leave" here and in other places in the Old Testament refers to the shift of an individual's devotion and loyalty from one person or group to another (cf. Deut. 28:20; 31:16; Ruth 2:11; Jer. 1:16; Hos. 4:10). The word "cleave" (*dābaq*; NIV, "be united") is especially prominent as a technical term in the covenant terminology of Deuteronomy (cf. Gen. 34:3; Deut. 10:20; 11:22; 13:4; 30:20; Josh. 22:5; 23:8; 1 Kgs. 11:2). So when a man leaves his father and mother and cleaves to his wife, he is abandoning one loyalty and beginning another. That the husband's loyalty to his wife (and the wife's to her husband) is to be exclusive of all others is also emphasized in the Old Testament. The prophets employ the marriage metaphor to show that Israel's covenant relationship with Yahweh excluded all other gods (Jer. 31:32; Hos. 13:4; cf. Exod. 20:1–6).

Marriage Covenants Are Established by Vows and Include Obligations

Further reinforcement that marriage is a covenant comes in the final statement in Genesis 2:24 that the man and the woman "will become one flesh." This is an abbreviated reference to the pledge of loyalty that Adam had just made to Eve, with God as his witness: "This is now bone of my bones and flesh of my flesh" (Gen. 2:23a). In biblical times, an oath or a vow was the main ingredient in establishing a covenant between two people or groups. God is actually called on to act as "the enforcer" of the covenant,[4] and Adam's words in Genesis 2:23a are his pledge to God to put Eve first in his life. If we fill in the details of Adam's vow, he is saying, "I hereby invite you, God, to hold me accountable to treat this woman as part of my own body."[5] This highlights the gravity of the vows marriage partners make before Almighty God. The teaching of Genesis 2:23–24 is what prompted Paul to say to husbands in Ephesians 5:28, "In this same way [that Christ sacrificially loved the church and was willing to die for her], husbands ought to love their wives as their own bodies. He who loves his wife loves himself." God is invoked at wedding ceremonies to witness the vows that couples make to one another, and to break such vows is to invite God's displeasure (cf. Exod. 20:7).

Marriage Covenants Can Be Broken

So if Scripture indicates that marriage is a covenant (cf. Ezek. 16:8, 60; Mal. 2:10–16) to which God is a witness (Gen. 31:50; Mal. 2:14), just how permanent are biblical covenants? The marriage relationship should not be viewed as on a par with the seemingly permanent nature of the "new covenant," the covenant that God said he would never break with his people (Jer. 31:31–34). While there is indeed a relationship between biblical marriage law and covenant concepts, the partners in the new covenant (God and fallen humanity) are not the same as the partners in a marriage covenant (two sinful but redeemed individuals with wills of their own).

Furthermore, covenants are *not* inherently unbreakable. Where Hebrew usage is concerned, "covenants may be both violated and dissolved—with both of these concepts expressed by the same underlying Hebrew expression which is customarily rendered 'broken' in most English versions."[6] As many have observed, Jesus' statement, "Therefore what God has joined together, let man not separate" (Matt. 19:6), does *not* mean "no one *can* separate," but rather it means "it *is* possible to separate, but you should not."[7]

Sexual Fidelity: A Crucial Covenant Obligation

What role, then, does sexual union play in the formation of the marriage covenant? The apostle Paul speaks of sexual relations in marriage as a mutual obligation that husbands and wives willingly render to one another (1 Cor. 7:2–5). Where did Paul get this idea?

Ancient Near Eastern marriage covenants or contracts included stipulations that were either written down or stated verbally before witnesses at a ceremony. These obligations could vary from one marriage to another. However, the most important covenant obligations were normally *not* written down.[8] This is because everyone already understood what they were. These consisted of "food, clothing and marital rights" (Exod. 21:10).[9] Indeed, sexual faithfulness is one of the stipulations that is rarely listed in these ancient Near Eastern marriage covenants, and thus one of the most important. This is confirmed by the fact that the death penalty for adultery *is* recorded throughout the ancient Near East and in the Old Testament itself (Lev. 20:10; Deut. 22:23–24; cf. Jer. 29:23).

The gravity of the sin of marital unfaithfulness in the eyes of both God and all humanity is evident throughout the Old Testament. Adultery was not only an offense committed against an injured husband but also an offense against God (cf. Gen. 20:6–10; 39:7). Adulterers are linked with murderers (Job 24:14–15) and treacherous men (Jer. 9:2) who misuse God's name (Jer. 29:23) and oppress widows (Mal. 3:5). We also read in the New Testament, "Let marriage be held in honor among all, and let the marriage bed be undefiled, for God will judge the sexually immoral and adulterous" (Heb. 13:4 ESV). If this is how God viewed a violation of the sexual exclusivity pledge in the marriage covenant, then it is most probable that Jesus, God's Son, would view that same sin similarly.

In summary, the Genesis 2:24 "one flesh" relationship that results from the marriage covenant ratified by vows before witnesses is *not* an indissoluble union. Rather, it is one that should preeminently *not* be violated, and a sexual sin like adultery—one that could receive the death penalty throughout the Old Testament world—is viewed as a major violation of the faithfulness vow that a husband and wife pledge to one another.

THE BIBLICAL RECOGNITION THAT ALL DIVORCES ARE *NOT* WRONG

One of the main reasons I believe that Jesus permitted divorce and remarriage at least for marital unfaithfulness is that Scripture itself makes a distinction between divorce with justifiable grounds and divorce without grounds.

Deuteronomy 24:1–4: Justifiable and Unjustifiable Divorces

Deuteronomy 24:1–4 is the central Old Testament text on divorce. Let's take a closer look:

> When a man takes a wife and marries her, if then she finds no favor in his eyes because he has found *a matter of indecency*[10] in her, and he *writes her a certificate of divorce* and puts it in her hand and sends her out of his house, and she departs out of his house, and if she goes and becomes another man's wife, and the latter man *hates her* and *writes her a certificate of divorce* and puts it in her hand and sends her out of his house, or if the latter man dies, who took her to be his wife, then her former husband, who sent her away, may not take her again to be his wife, after she has been defiled, for that is an abomination before the Lord. And you shall not bring sin upon the land that the Lord your God is giving you for an inheritance.
>
> Deuteronomy 24:1–4 ESV, emphasis mine

The specific ground for divorce mentioned in verse 1—literally, "a matter of indecency" (*ʿerwat dābār*)—was the point in dispute among the followers of the Jewish teachers Hillel and Shammai during Jesus' ministry. In fact, when Jesus was asked by some Pharisees, "Is it lawful for a man to divorce his wife *for any and every reason*?" (Matt. 19:3, emphasis added), they were asking him if he agreed with the popular Hillelite view encapsulated in the phrase "for any and every reason." Followers of Hillel placed no limits whatsoever on the Jewish husband's unilateral right to divorce his wife. The Shammaites, on the other hand, focused on the word "indecency" in the phrase in Deuteronomy 24:1 and limited the husband's right of divorce to "adultery."

Put simply, the law in Deuteronomy 24:1–4 states that a divorced woman who has contracted a second marriage may never subsequently be taken back by her first husband. In 1986, Raymond Westbrook highlighted a crucial distinction between the two divorces mentioned in this passage.[11] In the original marriage, the husband finds "a matter of indecency" in his wife and divorces her (v. 1), but the wife's second husband divorces her because he "hates" (NIV, "dislikes") her (v. 3). Westbrook did an extensive survey of marriage and divorce customs in the ancient Near East out of which the Old Testament laws arose, modified redemptively as they were by what God revealed to Moses. He also studied Jewish literature written after the close of the Old Testament that interpreted and applied the biblical teaching.[12]

Westbrook found that a phrase like "a matter of indecency" refers to a justifiable or valid ground for divorce; however, when "hates" or "dislikes" is added to the divorce formula, it "is used to show that the action arose from a subjective motive and without objective grounds to justify it—and for this reason is blameworthy."[13] This can be seen in Deuteronomy 24:3, where "hate" refers not to the divorce itself but to the subjective motive for the divorce. When a woman was subjectively or invalidly divorced, she was entitled to a financial settlement. She received back the dowry, which was a monetary or material gift given by the bride's father for her security in the marriage. Generally, she also would receive some compensation from her husband's resources (i.e., divorce payments). This means that divorce without objective grounds was costly for the husband. Divorce for "dislike," though legal, was frowned on by both the Old Testament and the surrounding ancient Near Eastern culture, as evidenced by the financial penalty imposed on the husband.

Malachi 2:16 Does Not Say That
God Hates All Divorce

This combination of "hate (NIV, "dislike") and divorce" is found not only in Deuteronomy 24:3 but also in Malachi 2:16 (aptly captured by the ESV): "For the man who hates and divorces, says the LORD, the God of Israel, covers his garment with violence, says the LORD of hosts. So guard yourselves in your spirit, and do not be faithless."[14]

Translations of Malachi 2:16, such as the NASB's "For I hate divorce, says the LORD, the God of Israel" (cf. KJV, NIV, NLT, NRSV), likely misconvey the sense of the original. In the Hebrew text, the subject of "he hates" is probably not Yahweh but the man, and so the reference is to an unjustifiable divorce (based on "hate").[15] This suggests that there is a justifiable divorce, however tragic, that God does not condemn. Most translations incorrectly convey the notion that God is against divorce of any kind.

The Deuteronomy 24:4 Prohibition Is Not
Directly Applicable Today

On several occasions, I have received calls from people asking whether the Deuteronomy 24:1–4 case law prohibits the restoration of a previous marriage after an intervening one. One man left his wife and three young children and married a coworker. His second wife was now divorcing him, and his first wife and children were willing to take him back. What should he do?

Before leaving this text, I would like to point out why I do not think this passage is still applicable in this way today.[16] Note that verse 3 links the second husband's divorce for "dislike" with what similarly happens if the second husband dies. This is because in both of these situations the wife retains the dowry. She is left financially well-off. Now we can see why the first husband would want to take his wife back: he wants to pad his wallet! Remember that he divorced his wife by asserting that he found in her "a matter of indecency." This short phrase was legal jargon for some socially recognized misconduct — either mishandling of her financial or household duties or sexual misconduct short of adultery. (Adultery, not divorce, was punished by death in the Old Testament [Lev. 20:10; Deut.

22:22].) So, whether his accusation was true or not, by asserting he found in her "a matter of indecency," the first husband managed to keep her dowry and was exempted from paying divorce money. Now that she is a wealthy widow or divorcée, he tries to take her back.

The reason Deuteronomy 24:4 says it would be an "abomination" for the husband to try to get back together with the wife again probably involves several transgressions of the law. For one, he may have put her away on trumped-up charges to begin with,[17] and this would make him a false witness (cf. Exod. 20:16; Deut. 5:20). For another, to remarry one's former wife for financial reasons is financial immorality. This puts the first husband on a par with a man who hires his wife out for prostitution![18]

None of the "restoration of previous marriage" cases that I have been asked about bear any similarity to the specific details of this Deuteronomy 24:1–4 case law. Thus, I do not believe that we should apply its prohibition to modern-day cases that bear only superficial similarities.

Deuteronomy 24:1 Was Read as a Command in Jesus' Time

I must clarify one last item about the bill of divorce mentioned in Deuteronomy 24:1. The Hebrew construction of Deuteronomy 24:1 is sufficiently ambiguous to allow two readings. One option is to read it like the NIV and all other modern translations ("and he writes her a certificate of divorce"). These suggest that the writing of the certificate of divorce is just one of the relevant facts of this case law laid out in verses 1–3; the actual law, then, is not found until verse 4. The other option is to read it like the KJV ("then let him write her a bill of divorcement"), which would mean that Moses *commanded* the giving of the bill of divorce. This is how the Jewish teachers whom Jesus debated read this law: "It has been said, 'Anyone who divorces his wife must give her a certificate of divorce'" (Matt. 5:31; cf. Matt. 19:7; Mark 10:3).[19] First-century Jews believed that Moses commanded the giving of a certificate of divorce, and that this command included grounds for divorce ("a matter of indecency"). The debate over justifiable grounds is precisely where the followers of Hillel and Shammai differed. They must have heard that Jesus was a bit more conservative than either of them, so they used this debated point as the question by which they hoped to trap him.

"DIVORCE" IN THE FIRST CENTURY WAS
SYNONYMOUS WITH THE RIGHT TO REMARRY

The most important reason for believing that Jesus and Paul would have sanctioned remarriage after divorce under specified exceptions is the very meaning of "divorce" in the minds of first-century readers. Simple separation without the possibility of remarriage was unheard-of in both Jewish and Roman marriage law. Though this became the traditional Catholic view of Jesus' teaching and is a view also held by a minority of evangelicals, there were, in fact, no religious sects in the first century that prohibited remarriage after divorce. The whole purpose of obtaining a divorce was to be freed up to remarry. This is what the Jewish bill of divorce made abundantly clear: "Behold, you are free to marry any man."

There were, however, cases in which divorce was judged as legitimate or illegitimate, valid or invalid, justifiable or unjustifiable, depending on the offense of one's marriage partner or the frivolous reasons for the divorce. Invalid divorces in Jewish marriage law resulted in financial penalties for the man; valid divorces resulted in financial penalties for the woman. Everyone agreed that a Jewish wife could be justifiably divorced, *and should be* (cf. Matt. 1:19) if she had committed adultery. However, a Jewish wife could be legitimately divorced for other reasons too, especially if she transgressed the law of Moses and Jewish custom. Here are some examples:

LEGITIMATE REASONS FOR DIVORCE (KETUBAH 7:6)
- giving a husband untithed food
- uttering a vow and not fulfilling it
- going out in public with her hair unbound
- speaking with any man in public

We think that divorcing one's wife because she goes out in public with her hair uncovered is strange or petty, but the scandalous cultural equivalent in our day would be a Christian wife who goes downtown wearing sexually provocative clothing to flirt with men when her husband is out of town.

So the first-century Jewish wife who was guilty of some socially recognizable offense against the marriage contract was divorced and forfeited her dowry. (As noted above, the dowry was the financial package that a woman's father sent with her into the marriage. It provided for her future in the event of her husband's death or divorce without just cause.) However, almost never was a divorcée or the one who initiated divorce prohibited from remarrying.[20]

Though Jesus was neither legalistic nor loose in his interpretation of the Old Testament law, we know that he saw the marriage relationship as far more binding than did his contemporaries. The limitations he placed on divorce and remarriage shocked even his disciples (Matt. 19:10). No doubt he discounted the vast majority of the grounds for divorce that his contemporaries took for granted. For certain he rejected *all* of the frivolous or illegitimate grounds for divorce practiced by Jewish males. However, the reason we cannot say that he rejected *all* justifiable grounds for divorce and remarriage is that Matthew informs us otherwise. As noted above, the Old Testament passage the Pharisees asked Jesus to comment on distinguishes between valid and invalid divorces. Not only this, but Matthew's account of the question Jesus was asked and the response he gave shows that he sided with the most conservative Jewish teacher's interpretation of that debated Old Testament text.

JESUS' TEACHING AS RECORDED BY MATTHEW

Today, when I hear about the publication of a new book by an up-and-coming New Testament scholar, I want to know where he or she comes out on hotly debated points of biblical interpretation. This is especially the case if their exegetical results have a significant impact on how we live our lives. The Pharisees were no different. That is why they asked Jesus in Matthew 19:3 (NRSV, emphasis added), "Is it lawful for a man to divorce his wife *for any cause*?" They not only wanted to know where Jesus stood on the new "no fault" divorce popularized by the Hillelites; they also hoped to discredit him. The following citations from Matthew and the Mishnah reveal that Jesus was fully conversant with every detail of the debate over grounds for divorce within first-century Judaism:

> [Jesus says,] "It has been said, 'Whoever divorces his wife, let him give her a certificate of divorce.' But I say to you that everyone who divorces his wife, *except for a matter of unchastity* [*parektos logou porneias*], causes her to commit adultery; and whoever marries a divorced woman commits adultery."
>
> Matthew 5:31–32, my translation

> "And I [Jesus] say to you, whoever divorces his wife, *except for unchastity* [*mē epi porneia*], and marries another commits adultery."
>
> Matthew 19:9 NRSV

> The School of Shammai say: A man should not divorce his wife unless he found in her a matter of indecency (*dᵉbar ᶜerwāh*), as it is said: *For he finds in her an indecent matter* (*ᶜerwat dābār*). And the School of Hillel say, Even if she spoiled his dish, since it says, *For he finds in her an indecent matter* (*ᶜerwat dābār*) [allowing divorce on the grounds of any "matter" because the text contains both the words "indecent" and "matter"].[21]
>
> Mishnah *Gittin* 9:10

Jesus' Words Echo First-Century Legal Jargon about Divorce

Recall that the Hillelites emphasized the word "matter" in the "a matter of indecency" phrase from Deuteronomy 24:1. They said that it covered all other grounds for divorce and could be used by anyone. The Shammaites, however, emphasized the word "indecency" and understood the word to mean "adultery." Though a Hillelite court had other means of discouraging hasty divorce, it did not require any evidence of grounds for divorce, and this made divorce much easier. Still, husbands who initiated "no fault" divorces were financially penalized.[22] The Shammaites, in contrast, would require evidence of unfaithfulness, and if proven in a messy court battle, the wife could be divorced and would lose the financial package (*kethubah*) that came with her into the marriage. Thus, the Hillelite "any cause" divorce quickly became the preferred form utilized by virtually all Jews, even before AD 70.[23]

Since the "any cause" legal terminology in the Pharisees' question in Matthew 19:3 reflects the Hillelite interpretation of "a matter of indecency" in Deuteronomy 24:1, it is highly probable that the "except for unchastity" clause in Matthew 19:9 reflects the Shammaite "nothing but indecency" (i.e., adultery) interpretation of the same.[24] Groundbreaking work on the Jewish backgrounds to Jesus' teaching on divorce now appears to confirm this conclusion.[25]

Interpreters have long recognized that the way the exception clause is worded in Matthew 5:32 ("except for a matter of unchastity") is the virtual equivalent of the way the Shammaites reworded the corresponding Hebrew phrase in Deuteronomy 24:1 ("a matter of indecency"). However, the Shammaite position was summarized in the rabbinic literature in two similar phrases, the second of which is worded almost identically to the phrase found in Matthew 19:9! So in both passages Jesus is using wording similar to that of the Shammaites in the same context in which they used it. If language means anything, we can be sure that Jesus had the same ground for divorce in mind that the Shammaites did when they employed these words.[26]

Jesus Says Hillelite "Any Cause" Divorces Are Invalid

So what is Jesus saying? Note that this is Jesus' answer to the question about "any cause" divorces the Pharisees put to him in Matthew 19:3. Jesus makes it clear that he rejects the Hillelite "any cause" divorces; for him, they are invalid. He is saying that whoever remarries after a Hillelite divorce is committing adultery! Not only that, but everyone would have recognized that the exception clause in Matthew 19:9 is identical to Shammai's interpretation of "a matter of indecency" in Deuteronomy 24:1. Thus, where Deuteronomy 24:1 is concerned, Jesus limits justifiable grounds for divorce to adultery.

Valid or legitimate divorces included the right to remarry, and *no one* in the first century denied remarriage to innocent victims of divorce.[27] If Jesus had intended to convey this, as the no-remarriage view maintains, he would have been using the word for "divorce" (*apolyein*) with a different meaning than that used by any of his contemporaries. His hearers never would have understood his point. If Jesus were changing the meaning of "divorce" to "simple separation only, without the right to remarry"—something he could well have done—Matthew's record of this interchange would have had to make this point much clearer. A valid divorce included the freedom to remarry, and everyone agreed with the Shammaites that adultery was justifiable grounds for divorce.

Jesus' "Ground" Was the Same as Shammai's, But His Focus Was Redemptive

So if Jesus employs a phrase that would, like Shammai's, allow remarriage after a valid divorce brought on by a spouse's marital unfaithfulness, how does his position differ from Shammai's? Jesus' divorce sayings were made within a sociocultural matrix where Jewish law nearly *mandated* divorce for sexual unfaithfulness and *prohibited* a wife from ever returning to her husband after she had been unfaithful.[28] Jesus challenges both of these notions and *encourages* offended spouses to forgive and take back unfaithful mates who are repentant. Remember that Jesus' contemporaries thought an adulteress deserved death (John 7:53–8:11); Jesus, however, showed mercy to the woman and told her to sin no more. Jesus also taught his disciples to forgive in ways they never would have thought possible (Matt. 18:21–35). Whereas a first-century Jewish husband would probably want to divorce an unfaithful wife (cf. Joseph's response to Mary in Matt. 1:19), Jesus' teaching in Matthew suggests that this is not commanded or even encouraged, but only permitted. In the sixth antithesis in the Sermon on the Mount ("Love your enemies and pray for those who persecute you, that you may be sons of your Father in heaven" [Matt. 5:44–45]), Jesus asks "his followers to do something that the Mosaic law had not asked the people of Israel to do: love one's enemy."[29] Likewise, Jesus is asking his disciples to forgive transgressions of the marriage covenant in order to preserve the marriage.

I am convinced that Jesus' goal would parallel Yahweh's relentless pursuit of unfaithful Israel throughout the Old

Testament and that just as God would try to save a marriage at all costs, so should God's people. Thus, the exception clause means that marriages *may* still be kept together even if the sin of immorality occurs. A repentant spouse should be forgiven and received back (cf. also the model of the prodigal son's father in Luke 15:11–32).

Jesus' divorce saying, "I tell you that anyone who divorces his wife, except for marital unfaithfulness, and marries another woman commits adultery" (Matt. 19:9), was radical. His stunned disciples reacted by saying, "If this is the situation between a husband and wife, it is better not to marry" (v. 10). There are two possible explanations for this stunned response. Jesus either prohibited *all remarriage after every divorce*, even divorce for sexual immorality, or he limited valid grounds for divorce and remarriage to a divorce that took place because of unrepentant sexual immorality. I believe the latter is more likely because the disciples, like nearly everyone else at the time, would have held to the Hillelite position, not the Shammaite position.[30] They had just heard Jesus say that Hillelite "any cause" divorces were illegitimate and that whoever remarries after such an invalid divorce commits adultery! This would have been shocking to first-century Jews, suggesting that Jesus' view is stricter than Shammai's—the radical love of God does unexpected things, like forgiving the seemingly unforgivable—and adequately explains the disciples' incredulous reaction in Matthew 19:10 to Jesus' saying in verse 9.[31]

WHY DO MARK AND LUKE OMIT THE EXCEPTION CLAUSE?

One major question remains: Why are the exception clauses absent from Mark and Luke's gospels? The sayings in both Mark 10:11–12 and Luke 16:18 give the impression that under no circumstances would divorce or remarriage ever be possible, so how should we read them?

First, note that it was the Pharisees who asked Jesus where he stood on the matter of divorce (Matt. 19:3; Mark 10:2). The response Jesus made was not addressed to friendly disciples who wanted to know how they could please God. Craig Blomberg's warning underscores this point: "The specific historical background that informed this debate, the particular way in which the question is phrased, and the unscrupulous motives behind the Pharisees' approach all warn us against the notion that Jesus was comprehensively addressing all relevant questions about marriage and divorce."[32]

Evangelical scholars who defend the view taken in this chapter understand Jesus' pronouncement in one of two ways. Some say that Jesus is using exaggeration or overstatement to make his point. Such statements always need qualification. This is very plausible because the Gospels emphasize that Jesus referred to himself as a prophet (Matt. 13:57), taught as a wise man (Matt. 12:38–42), and spoke out powerfully against the religious hypocrisy and injustices he observed (Matt. 23). Therefore, if Jesus wanted to drive home a particular point in the midst of a hostile audience, "his omission of any qualification may be understandable."[33]

Others are more comfortable identifying Mark and Luke's exceptionless saying as "a generalization which admits of certain exceptions."[34] New Testament scholars note that elsewhere in the Gospels (cf., e.g., Matt. 9:15; 19:21; esp. 13:57), we do not try to turn Jesus' sayings into exceptionless absolutes, so why should we do so in Matthew 19:9 or Mark 10:11–12?[35]

There is yet a third way to answer the question of why Mark and Luke omitted any reference to the exception for adultery that is explicit in Matthew. Perhaps they did so because the exceptions were obvious and well known to the original audience. No one in the first century prohibited divorce altogether, not even the strict Jewish Essene sect at Qumran.[36] Matthew added these "phrases that encapsulated the positions of the Hillelites and Shammaites respectively," not because he wanted to soften Jesus' absolute prohibition of divorce (as in the older critical view), but because he could no longer assume that his readers would automatically supply what was originally present[37] (assuming that Matthew was written later than Mark).

Instone-Brewer offers a helpful modern-day analogy:

> If someone asked in a modern church context, "Do you believe in the Second Coming?" there would be no necessity to add the phrase "of Jesus Christ." Strictly speaking, the question is nonsense without this additional phrase, but the question is perfectly acceptable because everyone

would mentally add the phrase "of Jesus Christ." Similarly, if someone asked, "Should women have equality?" it would be unnecessary to add the phrase "in employment and education." However, if the question had been asked a century ago, the implied additional phrase would have been "in voting rights." Thus, a good historian who was reporting such a debate would add the phrase "in voting rights," even though it is likely that the original questioner omitted it. This is equivalent to Matthew's addition of the phrase "for any matter" [NIV, "for any and every reason"] for the sake of his readers, who were no longer entirely familiar with the terms of this debate within rabbinic Judaism.[38]

We also mentally assume exceptions to sayings of Jesus like those found in Matthew 5:28: "But I tell you that anyone who looks at a woman lustfully has already committed adultery with her in his heart"; we add "except for his wife." Where Matthew 5:22 is concerned, "But I tell you that anyone who is angry with his brother will be subject to judgment," we assume Jesus meant if someone is angry "without cause."[39] Thus, when it comes to the core form of Jesus' divorce saying, "Whoever divorces his wife and marries another commits adultery" (Matt. 5:31–32; 19:9; Mark 10:10–12; Luke 16:18), the only assumption that first-century readers would bring to make sense of it is the assumption that the divorce was not valid. Matthew's "except for [a matter of] indecency" (NIV, "except for marital unfaithfulness") makes this assumption explicit. What is important to note for our purposes is that the intent of Jesus' teaching on divorce and remarriage is essentially the same, no matter which of the above three approaches is adopted.

PAUL'S EXCEPTIONAL SITUATION IN 1 CORINTHIANS 7:15

The apostle Paul encountered a problem at Corinth that Jesus never had to face in his earthly ministry. The preaching of the gospel resulted in the conversion of just one of the partners in marriage (1 Cor. 7:12–16). Paul, under the inspiration of the Spirit (7:40b; 14:37), makes it clear that the believing partner is not to divorce his or her unbelieving mate (7:12–14); but what if the unbeliever is unwilling to put up with his or her spouse's newfound faith and takes off? Paul writes: "But if the unbeliever leaves, let him do so. A believing man or woman is not bound [*ou dedoulōtai*, from *douloō*] in such circumstances; God has called us to live in peace" (v. 15).

The most natural reading of the exception Paul makes in this situation is that it frees or "looses" the believer from the obligations of his or her marriage covenant. It points to a valid or legitimate divorce. In fact, one expert in first-century culture and language noted that "if Paul meant that remarriage was not permitted, he said precisely the opposite of what he meant."[40]

Several good scholars argue that Paul does not here address the question of remarriage. However, there are some compelling reasons for adopting the majority view that Paul's "a believing man or woman is not bound in such circumstances" indicates that the believer is free to consider remarriage when abandoned by the unbelieving spouse. Let's consider the language Paul uses.

The essential formula in the Jewish bill of divorce was "you are free to marry any man" (*m. Giṭ.* 9:3). Paul's *negative* formulation in 1 Corinthians 7:15 ("A believing man or woman is not bound in such circumstances") makes precisely the same point. Given Paul's Jewish background, a good case can be made that he envisions the remarriage of the deserted party if he or she so chooses. Yet there is even more evidence that Paul's teaching in 1 Corinthians 7 makes use of the freedom language used in the Jewish bill of divorce. Jews in Graeco-Roman Palestine wanted to see their women married to fellow Jews, not to Gentiles. A line from a Jewish divorce deed at Wadi Murabba'at (dated to AD 71) differs in one key place from the formula laid down in the Mishnah: "You are free for your part to go and become the wife of any *Jewish* man that you wish."[41] Paul employs this same line from the standard Jewish divorce certificate—"Behold, thou art free to marry any man" (*m. Giṭ.* 9:3)—in 1 Corinthians 7:39, where he gives instructions to widows: "A wife is bound [*dedetai*, from *deō*] to her husband as long as he lives. But if her husband dies, *she is free to be married to whom she wishes, only in the Lord*" (ESV, emphasis added). The only difference between Paul and his Jewish contemporaries is that he substitutes "in the Lord" for the first-century Jewish divorce certificate's "any Jewish man."

So what's the point? Why would Paul quote Jewish divorce certificate language with reference to a widow's freedom to remarry? The clue to Paul's reasoning is probably found in a passage in later rabbinic writings. Rabbi Ashi (d. AD 427) attempted to prove that even a childless widow was free to remarry whomever she wanted. He reasoned that "if a divorce gave a woman complete freedom to marry whomever she wished, then widowhood would give her the same freedom."[42] From the language Paul employs in both 1 Corinthians 7:15 and 7:39, it appears that he, too, reasoned that if a divorcée had this freedom to remarry, then so would a widow! Paul assumes that victims of valid divorces have the right to remarry.

That Paul sanctions the remarriage of the deserted believer here in 1 Corinthians 7:15 helps confirm our argument that Matthew's exception clause functions in a similar fashion.[43] What Paul is doing in 1 Corinthians 7:15 also reinforces our point that Mark and Luke's records of Jesus' divorce sayings were never intended to be taken as absolute statements that admit of no exceptions.

NO-REMARRIAGE VERSES: 1 CORINTHIANS 7:39; ROMANS 7:2-3; 1 CORINTHIANS 7:10-11?

No-remarriage proponents make much of Paul's directive in 1 Corinthians 7:39, where he tells a widow she may remarry after the death of her spouse, and of his illustration in Romans 7:2-3, where he notes that a woman will be called "an adulteress" if she marries again before the death of her husband. We also hear that Paul must not have known about Matthew's exception clause when he dealt with the case of divorce among two believers in 1 Corinthians 7:10-11. He writes, "To the married I give this command (not I, but the Lord): A wife must not separate from her husband. But if she does, she must remain unmarried or else be reconciled to her husband. And a husband must not divorce his wife." In response (and in all fairness), one should at least admit the possibility that Paul did *not* have in view divorce resulting from adultery or desertion by an unbeliever when he made any of these statements. Cogent arguments exist to support this point.[44]

We know that Paul was addressing a situation at Corinth where one group of believers advocated sexual license (1 Cor. 6:12–20) and another group advocated sexual abstinence. The latter group lived by the motto "it is good for a man not to have sexual relations with a woman" (7:1b TNIV). Paul, for the most part, is correcting the abuses of this ascetic party in chapter 7. They were trying to force their views of sexual abstinence on (1) those currently married (vv. 2–7); (2) those formerly married, i.e., widows and widowers (vv. 8–9, 39–40); (3) those pledged to be married (vv. 25–28, 36–38); and (4) the never-before-married (vv. 29–35). This is why Paul has to say twice to those engaged to be married that it is not a sin to marry (vv. 28, 36). If anything, divorce is taking place because of the absence of sexual relations!

Corinth was subject to Roman law, and under that system either the husband or the wife could initiate the divorce simply by walking out. No cause had to be alleged, and no ratification by any outside authority was necessary. Most likely, some of the believers at Corinth had already made use of the Roman "divorce by separation." So when Paul tells them to remain unmarried or else be reconciled (v. 11), he must be assuming this is an invalid divorce. They should not consider themselves divorced at all.[45]

OTHER LEGITIMATE GROUNDS?

Might there be additional legitimate grounds for dissolving a marriage?[46] Here one must be cautious. Some believe that physical and emotional abuse justifies divorce, and I am sympathetic with this position.[47] Even when I held my former no-remarriage view, I taught that in a home where a parent was abusing the children or where a spouse was being physically or psychologically abused, common ethical sense dictates that Jesus would not require the oppressed party to stay. However, incompatibility and fits of anger would not fit under the banner of *porneia* or desertion. Also, provision for a spouse's food, clothing, and housing, like affection, communication, spiritual leadership, and a host of other qualities, are, no doubt, important requirements in marriage; but failures in these matters may not automatically justify divorce.

APPLYING THIS VIEW IN TODAY'S CHURCH

What, then, do the two exceptions for divorce and remarriage in the majority view have in common, and how should we seek to apply the findings of this chapter in our churches today?[48] Both sexual immorality and desertion are violations of marriage as a covenant (cf. Gen. 2:24—"leave and cleave" and "become one flesh"). Sexual immorality is a betrayal of the sexual faithfulness and exclusivity that are expected of the marriage partners; desertion is an abdication of the mutual physical, financial, emotional, and spiritual support that is pledged to one another as covenant partners (cf. Exod. 21:10–11; 1 Cor. 7:3–5; Eph. 5:25–32). In the case of the genuine exceptions, after innocent parties have made all reasonable attempts to save the marriage, neither the church nor mission agencies should stigmatize one's subsequent decision to remarry.

How Long Do I Wait?

On the view taken in this chapter, major questions facing those whose spouses have violated their marriage covenant and have not yet remarried are, "What do you mean by 'all reasonable attempts?'" "How long do I wait?" "When is enough, enough?" On the one hand, those with overly sensitive consciences may wait longer than necessary to decide to remarry. We *should* take seriously the call to model the forgiveness we received from Christ at the cross (Eph. 4:32; cf. Matt. 18:22; Luke 17:4). We *should* seek to imitate our merciful and patient heavenly Father as his beloved children (Matt. 5:48; Eph 5:1–2). Jesus *did* show mercy to the woman caught in adultery without condoning her sin (John 8:11a); but he also called her to a life of righteousness: "Go now and leave your life of sin" (v. 11b). If repentance is not forthcoming from the one who broke his or her marriage vows, after repeated attempts at reconciliation and in time God may unexpectedly and providentially bring another godly marriage partner into one's life. This, I think, is an indication that "enough is enough."

On the other hand, some may not pray and wait long enough for a spouse's potential turnaround. One family friend was somewhat eager to be divorced by her nominally "Christian" husband and inappropriately initiated it herself due to the lack of responsibility he manifested in their home. She remarried rather quickly, and her second marriage did not turn out to be what she expected at all. To her dismay, within a year her first husband got serious about his faith and his life was transformed, and she knows she would be much happier if she could get back together with him. Yet there is no biblical basis for her doing so.

What My Wife and I Learned about Who Is at Fault

Over the years, my wife and I have housed three different mothers and their children for several months at a time, either as a result of divorce or in an attempt to help facilitate reconciliation with their spouses. If we've learned anything from this, it is that our initial judgments about who was at fault in the relationship were almost the opposite of what was really going on. In one case, the wife had left her husband and three children and was living with another man she had met through work. Over a five-month period, she moved back and forth between her family and her "lover" two or three times. The last time she did this, her husband, who went to our church and attended my Sunday school class, warned her that if she were to leave again, he would never take her back.

We took the initiative to call his wife—we knew her through her children—and found her ready to follow the Lord (so we thought). We offered her a place to live, in the hope that reconciliation could take place. During the four months she lived with us, her husband met a divorcée, who also attended my Sunday school class. After about two months of seeing each other, they set a wedding date. We had thought we were on the way to helping him reconcile with his wife. Finally, one day at church he said to me, "I know what you're trying to do, Bill, and it won't work." He was so adamant in what he had decided to do that he moved up the wedding date without telling anyone.

As a member of the elder board at the time, I thought about what we should do. Church discipline crossed my mind, but I had to ask myself how many times I had gone to visit him after his wife moved out. How often had I called to see how he was doing? How many times had we offered to take his kids when he had to go out of town on business? (We had a few times.)

Could I take part in disciplining someone with whom I barely had a relationship—someone I saw once a week in my Sunday school class and with whom I had not followed the earlier steps of the church restoration process (Matt. 18:15–18)? Had I sought to disciple him and go to the Word with him to investigate what he should do? No, I had to say that I had not. So now I was compelled to think about how our church would continue to minister to this to-be-married pair of divorced persons. The one thing he told me he hoped would not happen if he remarried is that he would be cut off from our church. Our church was the only one he felt comfortable attending. He wanted a place where his children and his wife-to-be's children could hear God's Word taught. Would we cut off the opportunity to minister to him and his blended family?

I learned some other valuable lessons from all of this. First, I now see that this man knew the character of his repeatedly unfaithful wife better than we did. I'm not sure she ever really intended to reconcile with him. I have learned that appearances are deceiving and that I cannot judge someone based solely on those appearances.

Second, I learned that it is not up to me to decide when someone else's marriage should end or should be healed. Only the wronged spouse in a relationship should make that decision.

Finally, I'm saddened to think that my actions caused this man to remarry quietly in another church, when the teaching of Jesus would have permitted him to do so openly and without shame. At one point, he went well beyond what most men would be willing to do: he was willing to take her back, even after he learned that she had gotten pregnant by the other man; but then she moved out—for the last time.

Jesus and Those Who Remarry after an Invalid Divorce

What would Jesus say about those who remarry after an invalid divorce? I agree with this observation of Instone-Brewer:

> There is nothing to suggest that Jesus asked anyone to separate from the second husband or wife if one had remarried after an invalid divorce. Technically the marriage was adulterous, but if this was applied literally,

then there would be huge confusion and disruption to people's lives and families. This is presumably why the divorce saying found its way into the Sermon on the Mount. Just as someone who hates his brother is not to be prosecuted for murder, so one who has remarried is not to be accused in court of committing adultery.[49]

The Sexual Needs of Divorced Persons

What about the sexual needs of divorced people? I am leery of appealing to verses like 1 Corinthians 7:9 ("It is better to marry than to burn with passion"), which Paul addresses to widowers and widows (vv. 8–9), as a biblical basis for remarriage because one's sexual needs are not being fulfilled. Where invalid divorces are concerned, Paul seems to say that believers are to remain unmarried or to be reconciled in these situations (vv. 10–11; cf. Matt. 5:32b; Luke 16:18b). Also, the Old Testament stories of Joseph and Potiphar's wife (Gen. 39) and David and Bathsheba (2 Sam. 11) imply that God has given us control over the sexual area of our lives. We are not slaves to bodily passions. Though even truly redeemed people are still selfish, sinful, and imperfect, new life in Christ and the power of the indwelling Holy Spirit make living above failure a reality for those who call Jesus Lord (cf. Rom. 6:1–23; Gal. 5:22–26). Further, my never-before-married single friends are quite suspicious of arguments that seek to justify remarriage primarily to satisfy unfulfilled sexual desires. Certainly, as a lesser of two evils, it would be better to remarry than to commit sexual immorality, but this raises other questions I cannot address here.

Should Divorced or Remarried People Serve in Church Leadership Positions?

Let me comment on one final implication of the Bible's teaching on divorce and remarriage as it applies to church leaders, namely, pastors/elders/overseers, deacons, and deaconesses. The most recent studies of "the husband of but one wife" requirement (1 Tim. 3:2, 12; Titus 1:6) argue that it is a typical ancient way of saying "faithful to one's marriage." Paul does not prohibit from church office those who, against their own wishes, have been abandoned or sexually betrayed, but those who are unfaithful to their marriage partner.[50] Thus, divorced persons should not automatically be excluded from leadership positions in the church, nor should those who have remarried after the very limited cases in which the New Testament permits remarriage after divorce (i.e., divorce with just cause).

SELF-ACTUALIZATION VERSUS COVENANT FAITHFULNESS

Some very good arguments can be made for a no-remarriage view of the biblical teaching on divorce and remarriage. However, the seriousness with which God and all of humanity view adultery as a violation of covenant faithfulness, and the leaving that reverses the cleaving when an unbeliever abandons his or her Christian spouse, make it highly probable that such actions constitute covenant breaking. Though we do indeed "already" have the "firstfruits" power of the Spirit in our lives, enabling us to live in accordance with God's standard of lifelong marriage, we have "not yet" been brought fully "into the glorious freedom of the children of God" that awaits us after Christ's return (cf. Rom. 8:18–25). I believe this is why many of those who argue that Jesus never permitted divorce or remarriage go on to say, in view of continued hardness of heart, that we should apply Jesus' teaching much as I've presented it in this chapter.

Both majority and minority views want to avoid extremes in their application of the New Testament teaching. Minority-view proponents may, sadly, prohibit what God would permit, and majority-view proponents may permit what God would prohibit and open the door to divorce even wider. The latter is the danger in a culture that emphasizes self-actualization, personal fulfillment, and "being true to oneself" rather than being true to the attendant commitments and obligations of one's marriage covenant. This is why I want to end with this final consideration:

> The church must recognize and teach that marriage is grounded not in *feelings* of love but in the *practice* of love. Nor is the marriage bond contingent upon self-gratification or personal fulfillment. The church has swallowed a great quantity of pop psychology that has no foundation in the biblical depiction of marriage....

When the marital union is rightly understood as a *covenant*, the question of divorce assumes a very different aspect. Those who have made promises before God should trust in God for grace sufficient to keep those promises, and they should expect the community of faith to help them keep faith, by supporting them and holding them accountable.[51]

A RESPONSE TO WILLIAM A. HETH

Gordon J. Wenham

It is an odd experience to have to critique colleagues' works in public! I am, of course, accustomed to commenting on students' papers in private. What makes this occasion even more unnerving is that over a number of years Bill Heth and I have corresponded, and eventually we wrote *Jesus and Divorce* together (or to be candid, he did most of the writing and I helped, mostly by offering comments on his text). But now I find myself opposing him. I am sorry to be in this situation, but I appreciate that the atmosphere in America on this issue is somewhat different from the atmosphere in the United Kingdom, where many in the mainline churches have resisted the idea that the New Testament permits remarriage after divorce. Thus, it is easier for me in the UK to stick my neck out on this matter than it is for an American. Furthermore, anyone who honestly investigates a complicated issue like this may well conclude that we dare not be too dogmatic. And then, last but not least, all of us in Western society have friends or relatives who have become divorced and have remarried. We know how they suffered in their first marriage, and now they have married again and have found a happiness they did not know in their first marriage; who are we to say that they are wrong and that God disapproves of their present arrangement?

All of us need to tread very tactfully in this area. So I sincerely hope that where I take issue with Bill and those who sympathize with him, they will not take it personally. Clarity demands simplicity; but simple, clear statements may seem harsh in print, whereas the right tone of voice would have conveyed a gentler message. I do, therefore, hope that readers, including Bill, will understand that I am trying to speak the truth in love, however far I fall short of that ideal.

MINOR POINTS WHERE I SEE THINGS DIFFERENTLY

Bill begins by describing Old Testament views of marriage. Here he is greatly indebted to the work of Gordon Hugenberger and Raymond Westbrook, two excellent scholars. In this area I basically agree with what he says. There are just a few minor points where I would take a different approach.

Bill appeals to Jeremiah 31 to argue that, under the new covenant, God would never break his covenant with his people. This is not what the text says is new about the new covenant; its novelty is that *Israel* will not break the covenant (31:32). Jeremiah is adamant that God has not broken his covenant with Israel and never will (31:35). Applying this to marriage, I ask: If the people of the new covenant are not going to break their covenant with God, and God for his part is not going to break it, is it not fitting that human marriage, which is supposed to mirror God's love for his people and vice versa, also should not be broken?

My next quibble with Bill is over his use of the ESV translation of Malachi 2:16: "For the man who hates and divorces ... covers his garment with violence" instead of the traditional "For I hate divorce,... and I hate a man's covering himself with violence." As one of the ESV translators, I can assure readers that there was no idea in the translators' minds that this meant Malachi approved of some divorces. This is one of the most difficult passages in the whole Bible to translate, so no one can be sure about what the text means precisely. However, along with Bill and Gordon Hugenberger, I do think the new translation is more probable than the earlier English translations. But it is unwise to build a case on this problematic text. From the narratives and laws of the Old Testament, I think it is plain that God tolerates some divorces but never approves of them. How could he, when one considers the disloyalty, vow breaking, and bitterness divorce often involves? But, as Jesus put it, "Moses permitted you to divorce your wives because your hearts were hard" (Matt. 19:8). This is not justifying or approving divorce, but tolerating it.

BILL'S TREATMENT OF THE NEW TESTAMENT

In his treatment of the New Testament texts, Bill reiterates several times the fundamental fallacy in the permissive position, namely, that first-century people all held that divorce entailed the right to remarry. Therefore, he argues that this is what Jesus and the New Testament writers assume as well. In my chapter I have tried to show why this is wrong. However, Bill does admit that in certain cases the ancient world did forbid remarriage after divorce (see n. 20, p. 98). An adulterous spouse, after being divorced, could not marry the third party with whom he or she had had an affair. This rule, if applied today, would rule out a very high proportion of second marriages, from the British heir to the throne on down. But neither Romans nor first-century Jews tolerated such unions.

Permissive interpreters are also forced to admit that Jesus did use the word *apolyein* ("divorce") in a sense different from usual first-century usage, where the separation is not justified. They understand Matthew 19:9 to say, "In the case of sexual immorality, whoever divorces his wife and marries another does not commit adultery; in other cases, whoever divorces his wife and marries another does commit adultery." In the second case, the man concerned has given his wife the divorce certificate, telling her that she is free to marry, but according to Jesus, though the law allows both parties to marry, to do so is to commit adultery. In other words, the divorce proceedings are ineffective: the divorced couple are still husband and wife in the eyes of God. John Murray (who, like Bill, allows divorce and remarriage for adultery or desertion), puts it clearly: "If the woman commits adultery by remarriage, this is so because she is still in reality the wife of the divorcing husband. And if so, the divorcing husband is still in reality the husband of the divorced woman and consequently may not marry another."[1]

Bill is aware of this chink in his armor as he discusses the passages in Mark 10 and Luke 16, but he does not make much of it. It is clear, though, on the permissive interpretation, that Jesus uses *apolyein* in two different senses. When it is used without the exception clause, it means "separate" (without the right to remarry). When it is used with the exception clause, *apolyein* means "divorce" (with the right to remarry). On the no-remarriage view, Jesus always means "separate" when he uses *apolyein*.

Some other points: Bill does not show why, on his reading of Matthew 19:10–12, Jesus goes on to speak about "eunuchs," people who do not marry, whereas on a no-remarriage view, Jesus' further comments arise naturally. Neither am I persuaded that Hillelite divorce "for any cause" was a first-century novelty. I think such divorce was allowed in Old Testament times and in earlier Near Eastern cultures. Repayment of the dowry was the means of discouraging "any cause" divorce from prebiblical to modern times in the Middle East. Bill's possible readings of 1 Corinthians 7, which he describes as "most natural" or "compelling," also fail to persuade me. I would allow that the texts he quotes might mean what he says they mean, but the evidence for taking them this way is far from compelling. I much prefer the interpretations we espoused in *Jesus and Divorce*.

DOES THE PERSON WITH THE MOST POINTS WIN?

This brings me to one final consideration. Anyone who reads books and articles about the Bible soon becomes aware that it is very difficult to know which arguments are right. Some years ago, two eminent New Testament scholars, E. P. Sanders and J. M. G. Barclay, argued that it was no good just counting arguments for and against a particular view but that all arguments should be weighed. If scholar A puts forward ten arguments in favor of a point of view and scholar B puts forward seven arguments against that view, it does not follow that A is right and B is wrong. B's arguments may be strong ones, while A's arguments may be weak. I think we need to discriminate between weak and strong arguments when it comes to the issue of remarriage after divorce.

Different people will evaluate the arguments differently, and where this occurs, we may well want to regard some arguments as weak, as merely possible rather than as probable or compelling. Into this iffy category, I put most of the interpretations offered by Bill (and Craig) with regard to the texts in

Matthew and Paul. Their interpretations could be right, but the no-remarriage view also makes sense and therefore *it* could be right. It is hard to know.

I think the no-remarriage view has three arguments that are stronger than any the permissives can offer. First, outside of Matthew's gospel, there are no texts that hint at remarriage after divorce as being a possibility. Second, in Matthew 19:3–12, only a no-remarriage view makes sense of the sequence of thought; it fits with the pattern of debate between Jesus and his opponents, and it explains why Jesus moves from speaking about divorce to "eunuchs," people who do not marry. Third, a no-remarriage view explains why the early church refused to sanction remarriage and often excommunicated those who did marry after divorce. A permissive interpretation of the New Testament texts has the impossible task of explaining how the early church came to adopt this stance when the surrounding cultures were permissive in this regard. Only someone with the authority of Jesus or Paul could have persuaded the early church to take such a countercultural stance. Some evangelicals may be reluctant to give so much weight to early church tradition, but our founding fathers, the great reformers, often appealed to the early church in support of their views. And in recent times we have done the same with regard to abortion. There are no New Testament texts that unequivocally ban abortion, though there are various ethical and theological texts that suggest that the New Testament writers would not have approved it. But early church writers are forthright on this subject, and we quote them freely in their condemnation of abortion. Is it not sensible to look at what the early church taught about divorce and remarriage too?

A RESPONSE TO WILLIAM A. HETH

Craig S. Keener

Responding to Bill Heth's argument here is both a joy and a trial. It is a joy because I am grateful for his courage in taking this position publicly, though it reverses the argument he had defended over the years. Bill and I have been dialogue partners on the issue for over a decade (including participating in a *Christianity Today* forum, where we represented opposing biblical views on remarriage). He has mentioned elsewhere that my book started him on the road to rethinking some of his argument (which may make me appear doubly reprehensible to our detractors!); more recent works by David Instone-Brewer and others finally convinced him to change his position.

A RARE REVERSAL

I have seen no scholar cited more often than Bill in favor of the no-remarriage position, so his reversal (in view of the many who still depend on his former case to prohibit remarriage) is significant. I would hope that even those who disagree with him will commend his humility and scholarly open-mindedness in being willing to rethink his argument, and his courage in breaking with a position that everyone (especially supporters of the no-remarriage position, many of whom are friends) expected him to defend. Such reversals are rare among scholars, especially when a scholar has traditionally been hailed as a position's leading defender.

Responding to Bill's argument is a trial, however, because it is difficult to know what to say when there is so little with which I disagree. His position, like that of David Instone-Brewer, whom he cites, is very close to my own in ... *And Marries Another*. The advantage of multiple-views books is that they can articulate various divergent positions on an issue; in practice, however, the individuals defending these positions may be nearer or further apart. Whereas my assignment forced me to explore other exceptions more pointedly and Bill's forced him to focus on the explicit biblical exceptions, our views do not seem far apart.

A LITTLE ELABORATING

In little, if any, of what follows am I contradicting what Bill has written; mostly I'm simply adding my own perspectives. I would contend that Jesus is at least *rhetorically* stricter than the Shammaites, who did not consider divorces on wider grounds illegal. (At least in some later sources, it is said that Shammaites broadened the category of "indecency" further than what we mean by "adultery"; attempts to seduce others [such as going out in public with uncovered hair] counted, even if no intercourse took place.) In practice, though, I would consider Jesus' claim of "adultery," which is harsher than normal Shammaite language on this issue, to be hyperbolic. This use of hyperbole is analogous to second-century rabbis calling sexual self-stimulation or lust adulterous (e.g., *b. Nid.* 13b; in the third century, cf. *Pesiq. Rab.* 24:2; *Lev. Rab.* 23:12), but without instituting actual legal sanctions, as in the case of intercourse.

Bill is correct that most people in this period would have followed the broader Hillelite position. This need not be because the school of Hillel was dominant in this period (tradition claims that Shammaites were dominant before the fall of Jerusalem) but because on this point Hillelites reflected the wider practice (attested, e.g., in Sir. 25:26). In any case, whatever view Jesus took could be used against him by proponents of a different view.

Bill notes three approaches to Jesus' tersest prohibition of divorce, namely, (1) it is hyperbole; (2) it is a generalized statement; or (3) the exception was already implicit in the statement and for cultural reasons did not always need to be stated. I believe that all three approaches are plausible; they are not mutually exclusive. Similarly, I would argue that 1 Corinthians 7:39 and Romans 7:2–3 are generalized statements and that the divorce issue could be taken for granted (especially since the Romans passage describes "the law"; cf. Deut. 24:1–4).

Bill is leery of appealing to the sexual needs of divorced people as grounds for remarriage. He is certainly right that the argument cannot depend on this; if God forbids remarriage, divorced Christians—like all single Christians (and married people when physical distance, infirmity, or the spouse's refusal makes intercourse impossible)—would need to control themselves sexually. If, however, remarriage is permitted, sexual desire would be no less a reason for a divorced person to marry than for a single person (cf. 1 Cor. 7:8–9, 27–28; Paul prefers singleness for any so gifted).

SOME NECESSARY EXTRAPOLATING

I think that Bill's case for the two explicit biblical exceptions is clear, and I anticipate that most readers will agree on this point. This is currently the least controversial position (at least among evangelicals) and is also the easiest position to defend from Scripture.

My assignment, extrapolating Scripture's principles to resolve questions not explicitly addressed in the biblical text, involves a more difficult interpretive approach (though most of us commonly employ it for various other issues). Yet if we are to grapple with issues that Scripture does not address explicitly (or even to apply Scripture's principles to our congregation's needs in our sermons), we must consider how to extrapolate such principles. This approach leaves more areas undefined than some people (including myself) feel comfortable with. (Unhappily, much of life proves more ambiguous than we feel comfortable with; while Scripture defines many issues for us explicitly, it does not define all of them.) We cannot avoid extrapolating principles, but it is sometimes a complex task to define how far to extrapolate particular principles (such as, in this case, protecting an innocent party) in view of other principles (such as, in this case, our Lord's prohibition of divorce).

Here I am not arguing against Bill, whose conclusions do not differ from mine. Toward the end of his chapter, he argues that we should not require separation for remarriages that spring from invalid divorces. Likewise, he expresses his sympathy for physical (and even emotional) abuse with regard to justifying a divorce, but he rejects incompatibility, fits of anger, lack of provision, and so forth as valid grounds for divorce. I cannot see any difference between the position I articulate in the next chapter and that for which Bill has sympathy. Here, therefore, I am simply taking the opportunity to explore the hermeneutical questions involved in pressing beyond the explicit biblical exception.

Paul makes an exception (analogous to but different from Matthew's exception) when a new issue comes up, which he apparently did not address in Corinth previously. If this issue hadn't come up, we would not have an explicit exception for abandonment. What, then, of issues that did not come up? What if physical abuse had come up? We do not have an explicit text that addresses the question, but if we follow the principle Paul follows (which, probably not coincidentally, agrees with Matthew's exception), we may guess that Paul would have treated a situation like abuse in the same way he responded to the situation of abandonment. (Most today allow divorce, or at least separation, for continued abuse, even if they do not allow remarriage. But if the understanding of "divorce" that Bill and I espouse is correct, permission to eventually remarry is, by definition, implied in the divorce.)

The text provides other principles that also offer some boundaries on the more restrictive side; for example, Paul explicitly disallows "spiritual incompatibility" as an exception (despite the existence of arranged marriages in his day). True exceptions dare not be excuses to escape a difficult relationship but rather occur when the other partner ruptures the marriage covenant against the nonoffending party's best efforts to preserve marriage. Like many principles, this one leaves us with some uncomfortably ambiguous pastoral situations in practice. In such ambiguous cases, pastoral sensitivity to the situation and to the Holy Spirit cannot be circumvented simply by an appeal to "established results" of biblical scholarship.

An old argument centers around the question of whether to allow only what the Bible allows, or to allow whatever it does not forbid. In an extreme form practiced only by a few, the former approach forbids cars and electricity; in an extreme form practiced by many, the latter approach is used to justify a range of behaviors (a pervasive example is watching unwholesome television programs when such behavior contravenes biblical principles about doing everything for God's glory, meditating on Christ, and so forth).

A sounder approach is to let Scripture's principles guide us to a deeper relationship with God that helps us discern what is consistent with biblical principles, even when we lack explicit biblical statements. Scripture invites us to hear God's heart and to desire what God desires. Without that heart, it is difficult to avoid the extremes of legalism and libertinism, of judging others too harshly and of justifying whatever appeals to our passions. May we have God's heart to work against the evil of divorce and injustice in marriages, while we also work for the healing of those broken by such acts.

Chapter 2: Remarriage for Adultery or Desertion

1. A 1992 *Christianity Today* readers' survey revealed that "the majority believe that fornication (73 percent) and desertion by a non-Christian spouse (64 percent) are two scriptural grounds for remarriage. At the same time, a significant minority believe Jesus taught that believers should not remarry after divorce (44 percent) and that God designed marriage to be permanent, and that remarriage constitutes adultery (44 percent). Less than four out of ten believe there may be reason for remarriage other than adultery or desertion. Those who have been divorced are more likely to accept other reasons" (Haddon Robinson, "CT Readers Survey: Sex, Marriage, and Divorce," *Christianity Today* [Dec. 14, 1992], 31).

2. See my "Another Look at the Erasmian View of Divorce and Remarriage," *JETS* 25 (1982): 263–72; "The Meaning of Divorce in Matthew 19:3–9," *Chm* 98 (1984): 136–52; "Divorce and Remarriage," in *Applying the Scriptures: Papers from ICBI Summit III*, ed. K. S. Kantzer (Grand Rapids: Zondervan, 1987), 219–39; "Divorce, but No Remarriage," in *Divorce and Remarriage: Four Christian Views*, ed. H. Wayne House (Downers Grove, Ill.: InterVarsity, 1990), 73–129; "The Changing Basis for Permitting Remarriage after Divorce for Adultery: The Influence of R. H. Charles," *TJ* 11 NS (1990): 143–59; "Divorce and Remarriage: The Search for an Evangelical Hermeneutic," *TJ* 16 NS (Spring 1995): 63–100; with Gordon J. Wenham, *Jesus and Divorce: Towards an Evangelical Understanding of New Testament Teaching* (London: Hodder & Stoughton, 1984; Nashville: Nelson, 1985; updated ed., Carlisle: Paternoster, 1997).

3. This chapter contains revised portions of my article "Jesus on Divorce: How My Mind Has Changed," *SBJT* 6 (Spring 2002): 4–29. Used by permission. I also want to thank Dr. David Instone-Brewer, Tyndale House, Cambridge, for the many email exchanges we shared and the way his work has influenced my own thinking on this subject recently.

4. See Gordon P. Hugenberger, *Marriage as a Covenant: Biblical Law and Ethics as Developed from Malachi* (Biblical Studies Library; Grand Rapids: Baker, 1998), 11–12, 193, 215.

5. Cited in Hugenberger, *Marriage as a Covenant*, 165.

6. Ibid., 3 n. 25; cf. David Instone-Brewer, *Divorce and Remarriage in the Bible: The Social and Literary Context* (Grand Rapids: Eerdmans, 2002), 1–19.

7. David Instone-Brewer, *Divorce and Remarriage in the Church: Biblical Solutions for Pastoral Realities* (London: Paternoster, 2003), 7. Cf. Craig L. Blomberg, "Marriage, Divorce, Remarriage, and Celibacy: An Exegesis of Matthew 19:3–12," *TJ* 11 NS (1990): 169–70; Bruce Kaye, "'One Flesh' and Marriage," *Colloq* 22 (1990): 51.

8. See Instone-Brewer, *Divorce and Remarriage in the Bible*, 8.

9. The distinctive contribution of Instone-Brewer's *Divorce and Remarriage in the Bible* is that he identifies two additional biblical grounds for divorce based on Exod. 21:10–11 (see his p. 102). Rabbinic sources classified these under two headings: material neglect and emotional neglect.

10. I am departing from the ESV here to pursue a more literal rendering of the Hebrew text in order to clarify a point.

11. Cf. Raymond Westbrook, "The Prohibition on Restoration of Marriage in Deuteronomy 24:1–4," in *Studies in the Bible 1986*, ed. Sara Japhet (ScrHier 31; Jerusalem: Magnes, 1986), 387–405. Both Hugenberger (*Marriage as a Covenant*, 79–81) and Instone-Brewer (*Divorce and Remarriage in the Bible*, 7) affirm Westbrook's findings on the distinction between the two divorces and the related financial penalties but find the unjust enrichment motivation only half correct. Neither Stephen Clark (*Putting Asunder: Divorce and Remarriage in Biblical and Pastoral Perspective* [Bryntirion, Bridgend, Wales: Bryntirion Press, 1999]) nor Alex R. G. Deasley (*Marriage and Divorce in the Bible and the Church* [Kansas City, Mo: Beacon Hill, 2000]) mention Westbrook in connection with their treatment of Deuteronomy 24:1–4.

12. Cf. also Judith R. Wegner, *Chattel or Person? The Status of Women in the Mishnah* (New York: Oxford Univ. Press, 1988), 80–86; Léonie J. Archer, *Her Price Is Beyond Rubies: The Jewish Woman in Graeco-Roman Palestine* (JSOTSup 60; Sheffield: Sheffield Academic Press, 1990), 173, 176–81.

13. Westbrook, "Prohibition on Restoration of Marriage," 402.

14. For the best defense of this translation, see Hugenberger, *Marriage as a Covenant*, 48–83. Instone-Brewer concurs (*Divorce and Remarriage in the Bible*, 7 n. 30). David Clyde Jones ("A Note on the LXX of Malachi 2:16," *JBL* 109 [1990]: 683–85) also points out, prior to Hugenberger (but not listed in Hugenberger's bibliography), that the LXX manuscripts א B A and Q witness to the interpretation favored here: "if you divorce out of hatred." Jones does not evidence familiarity with Westbrook and seems not to notice that the divorce for "a matter of indecency" in Deut. 24:1 differs from the one God justly condemns in Mal. 2:16 (cf. David Clyde Jones, *Biblical Christian Ethics* [Grand Rapids: Baker, 1994], 189–92).

15. Here is Hugenberger's paraphrase of Malachi 2:16: "If one hates and divorces [that is, if one divorces merely on the ground of aversion], says Yahweh, God of Israel, he covers his garment with violence [i.e., such a man visibly defiles himself with violence], says Yahweh of hosts. Therefore, take heed to yourselves and do not be faithless [against your wife]" (*Marriage as a Covenant*, 76).

16. At one point, I argued that the Deuteronomy 24:4 prohibition still applies (my *Jesus and Divorce*, 200–201), and some still do (cf. Clark, *Putting Asunder*, 183–84).

17. The phrase "after she has been defiled" (Deut. 24:4) involves the legal principle of estoppel and would be better translated "after she has been made to declare herself to be unclean." Cf. John H. Walton, "The Place of the *Hutqattel* within the D-Stem Group and Its Implications in Deuteronomy 24:4," *HS* 32 (1991): 12. Walton improves on Westbrook when he notes that "the law restricts the first husband because he forced her to publicize something that was embarrassing to her perhaps to achieve his own selfish ends" (14–15). Walton also points out, as I did in "Divorce, but No Remarriage" (p. 86), that Westbrook's interpretation is supported by Stephen A. Kaufman's brilliant analysis of "The Structure of the Deuteronomic Law," *Maarav* 1/2 (1978–79): 105–58.

18. Cf. David Instone-Brewer, "Deuteronomy 24:1–4 and the Origin of the Jewish Divorce Certificate," *JJS* 49 (1998): 233–34. Both Hugenberger (*Marriage as a Covenant*, 77 n. 144 point j.) and Instone-Brewer believe that the law of Deut. 24:1–4 wants to prohibit what may be called "legalized adultery" or "pimping."

19. Evidence for this is also found in the LXX translation of Deut. 24:1, in Philo (*Spec. Laws* 3.30), and in Josephus, the first-century Jewish historian (*Life* 426–27; *Ant.* 4.253).

20. The only exception would be a Roman law and a Jewish practice that forbade an adulterer from marrying the one with whom he or she had committed adultery, but not someone else.

21. I am using Instone-Brewer's translation (*Divorce and Remarriage in the Bible*, 111).

22. See Archer, *Her Price Is Beyond Rubies*, 177–78, 180.

23. Archer (*Her Price Is Beyond Rubies*, 218 n. 3) observes, "Only in instances when the husband's reason for divorce, if proven true, would exempt him from the obligation of *kethubah* payment ... , did he need to present his case to a court. In Joseph's case [Matt. 1:19], had he acted on his intent and proceeded in public, not only would he not have had to pay the *kethubah*, but he could also have charged Mary with adultery" (cf. Instone-Brewer, *Divorce and Remarriage in the Church*, 45–46, 134–35).

24. D. J. Moo ("Law," in *Dictionary of Jesus and the Gospels*, ed. J. B. Green and S. McKnight [Downers Grove, Ill.: InterVarsity, 1992], 455) notes that "Jesus' position is not far from that of his near-contemporary Shammai, and from Deuteronomy 24:1–4 as well" (cf. Heth and Wenham, *Jesus and Divorce*, 168).

25. Instone-Brewer's research well qualifies him to comment on this topic (cf. David Instone-Brewer, *Techniques and Assumptions in Jewish Exegesis before 70 CE* [TSAJ 30; Tübingen: Mohr, 1992]).

26. Cf. Instone-Brewer, *Divorce and Remarriage in the Bible*, 186. The Shammaite phrase equivalent to the wording of the exception in Matt. 19:9 appears in *Sifre Deut.* 269; *y. Soṭah* 1.2 (16b).

27. See C. S. Mann, *Mark: A New Translation with Text and Commentary* (AB 27; Garden City, N.J.: Doubleday, 1986), 388. Cf. R. H. Stein, "Divorce," in *Dictionary of Jesus and the Gospels*, 193; Craig Blomberg, *Matthew* (NAC; Nashville: Broadman, 1992), 111.

28. Cf. Marcus Bockmuehl, "Matthew 5.32; 19.9 in the Light of Pre-Rabbinic Halakah," *NTS* 35 (1989): 291–95 (see also Warren Carter, *Households and Discipleship: A Study of Matthew 19–20* [JSNTSup 103; Sheffield: Sheffield Academic Press, 1994], 56–89; A. Tosato, "Joseph, Being a Just Man," *CBQ* 41 [1979]: 547–51).

29. Moo, "Law," 456.

30. Archer (*Her Price Is Beyond Rubies*, 219) observes that "in the first century the Shammaites attempted to restrict the man's power of divorce to charges of adultery, but such was the strength of the ancient view that

the normally more progressive school of Hillel came out in opposition and declared that a man could divorce his wife for any cause."

31. Interestingly, Raymond F. Collins (*Divorce in the New Testament* [GNS 38; Collegeville, Minn.: Liturgical Press, 1992], 120–26), like Robert H. Gundry, follows the minority view on Matthew 19:10–12 (i.e., that Jesus' "not all can accept *this saying*" [v. 11] refers to Jesus' divorce saying in v. 9, not to the disciples' retort in v. 10) but believes that divine enablement to remain single is given to those who divorce or have been divorced for *reasons other than unchastity* (v. 9). Collins's exegesis is seconded by Richard B. Hays, *The Moral Vision of the New Testament* (Edinburgh: T&T Clark, 1996), 376–77 n. 17. Hays has a brief but excellent canonical synthesis of the biblical teaching on divorce and remarriage (pp. 361–76) after his survey of the gospel divorce texts and Paul (pp. 347–61).

32. Blomberg, *Matthew*, 289–90. Thus, Stein ("Divorce," 197) notes that it is quite unlikely we should treat "Jesus' words as if they were the objective, referential language of jurisprudence seeking to convey a legal precept."

33. Stein, "Divorce," 194.

34. Blomberg, "Marriage, Divorce, Remarriage, and Celibacy," 162.

35. Ibid., 162–63.

36. We now know that not even the strict Jewish Essene sect prohibited divorce or remarriage after divorce (cf. Craig S. Keener,... *And Marries Another: Divorce and Remarriage in the Teaching of the New Testament* [Peabody, Mass.: Hendrickson, 1991], 41; Instone-Brewer, *Divorce and Remarriage in the Bible*, 63–64, 66, 70–71).

37. Instone-Brewer, *Divorce and Remarriage in the Bible*, 134.

38. Ibid., 135–36.

39. Ibid., 153.

40. Keener, ... *And Marries Another*, 61.

41. Cited in Archer, *Her Price Is Beyond Rubies*, 131; cf. 220. For the text and translation of the deed, see her appendix 1 (p. 298). Cf. also Instone-Brewer, *Divorce and Remarriage in the Church*, 100.

42. Instone-Brewer, *Divorce and Remarriage in the Bible*, 209.

43. Hays (*Moral Vision of the New Testament*, 18) would refer to Paul's words in 1 Cor. 7:15 as "theology in progress." He finds it unlikely that Paul would categorically prohibit remarriage for the believers described in vv. 12–16; "rather he would invite them to engage with him in a process of discernment about how they could best serve God in the 'present necessity' (v. 26), in the time that remains" (p. 361).

44. On Rom. 7:2–3 and 1 Cor. 7:39, see John Murray, *Divorce* (Phillipsburg, N.J.: Presbyterian & Reformed, 1953), 78–95; Instone-Brewer, *Divorce and Remarriage in the Church*, 76–79; Clark, *Putting Asunder*, 201–2.

45. Cf. Instone-Brewer, *Divorce and Remarriage in the Church*, 66–67; Susan Treggiari, "Divorce Roman Style: How Easy and How Frequent Was It?" in *Marriage, Divorce, and Children in Ancient Rome*, ed. Beryl Rawson (Oxford: Clarendon Press, 1991), 31–46.

46. Blomberg (*Matthew*, 293), Jones (*Biblical Christian Ethics*, 202–3), Hays (*Moral Vision of the New Testament*, 372), Clark (*Putting Asunder*, 154–56), and Keener (*... And Marries Another*, 105) all answer this question in the affirmative.

47. Cf. Gary P. Liaboe, "The Place of Wife Battering in Considering Divorce," *Journal of Psychology and Theology* 13 (1985): 129–38.

48. Gordon Hugenberger observes in an email communication (Jan. 10, 2002), "In terms of their implications for marriage and divorce, the ancient world lumped together adultery and desertion ('you can't have me' is the standard expression in the law codes). Both were seen to justify divorce and cause the guilty wife to forfeit her dowry, for example."

49. Instone-Brewer, *Divorce and Remarriage in the Bible*, 183.

50. See esp. Keener, *... And Marries Another*, ch. 7 ("Can Ministers Be Remarried?—1 Timothy 3:2"); S. Page, "Marital Expectations of Church Leaders in the Pastoral Epistles," *JSNT* 50 (1993): 105–20; Keener, "Husband of One Wife," *AME Zion Quarterly Review* 109 (January 1997): 5–24. Jay E. Smith ("Can Fallen Leaders Be Restored to Leadership?" *BSac* 151 [1994]: 455–80) focuses on another related issue: Does sexual immorality permanently disqualify one from leadership? He concludes that the Pastoral Epistles' leadership qualifications are concerned with the current, not the past, status of a leader's character, that fallen leaders can be restored *if* both their lives and their reputations inside and outside (cf. Rom. 2:24) the church can be rehabilitated, but notes that this may be very difficult.

51. Hays, *Moral Vision of the New Testament*, 372. Hays's study has also had an impact on the chapter "Marriage and Divorce" in Glen H. Stassen and David P. Gushee, *Kingdom Ethics: Following Jesus in Contemporary Context* (Downers Grove, Ill.: InterVarsity, 2003), 271–89.

Chapter 2: A Response to William A. Heth
(Gordon J. Wenham)

1. John Murray, *Divorce* (Philadelphia: Presbyterian & Reformed, 1976), 25.

Chapter Three

REMARRIAGE FOR ADULTERY, DESERTION, OR ABUSE

REMARRIAGE FOR ADULTERY, DESERTION, OR ABUSE

Craig S. Keener

It is a privilege to share this volume with my co-contributors. I have long respected Gordon Wenham as one of the finest evangelical Old Testament scholars; William Heth is one of the most prodigious scholars on the biblical teaching on divorce and has long been a personal friend.

Although this chapter is pastoral in its focus, I am first of all a biblical scholar. Like my coauthors in this book, I have treated the pertinent texts more extensively in earlier writings. I did so especially in an earlier book on divorce[1] and in a more recent commentary on Matthew;[2] the exegetical questions also resurface in a recently published commentary on 1 Corinthians.[3] Those works provide much fuller documentation, references to other texts, and answers to objections I cannot address in this brief chapter.[4]

I have often argued that the Bible permits remarriage for the innocent party whose partner abandoned or proved consistently unfaithful to them (a position argued in this volume by Bill Heth).[5] In this chapter, however, I have the more difficult, though important, task of arguing for the possibility of remarriage beyond the explicit New Testament exceptions. I believe that the NT exceptions point us to principles that can guide us in some extreme situations the NT writers did not directly address. I argue that abuse is analogous to the sorts of circumstances the NT explicitly addresses; I also argue that remarriages remain true marriages in God's sight, hence that the church should work to preserve, and not to break up, such marriages. To bring new divorce into such marriages would compound the sin of divorce.

THE NEW TESTAMENT AND REMARRIAGE

The New Testament includes five or six passages that explicitly address the question of remarriage:

TOPIC	SCRIPTURE
Jesus' summary statement on the moral intention of the law	Matthew 5:32
Jesus' summary statement on the moral intention of the law	Luke 16:18
Jesus' debate with the Pharisees	Matthew 19:9
Jesus' debate with the Pharisees	Mark 10:11-12
Pastoral application by Paul	1 Corinthians 7:15
Pastoral application by Paul	1 Corinthians 7:27-28

However we interpret these texts, it is clear that all of them oppose divorce; yet it is noteworthy that four of these six texts allow exceptions.

Jesus warned that whoever remarries commits adultery (Matt. 5:32; 19:9; Mark 10:11–12; Luke 16:18). If he intended this statement literally, the new union is adulterous; hence sin occurs during every act of intercourse (not simply during the remarriage ceremony). In this case, we should not merely forbid divorced church members to remarry; we should regard their remarriages as adulterous unions and thus seek to break them up, even if the remarriages preceded their conversion. Most of us who have been pastors or are on ministry staffs of churches (or have otherwise served in church leadership) can imagine with horror the pastoral implications of this doctrine. (It would also be surprising, if this had been Paul's practice in Corinth, that Paul did not have to address the subject in his correspondence there. Given what we know about divorce in Greek and Roman urban culture in Paul's day,[6] many of his converts must have already been remarried at the time of conversion.)

A few churches actually try to implement this practice literally. After one couple I know about came to Christ, the wife decided she had sinned in marrying her current husband because she had been divorced from another husband many years earlier. Over the next decade, she insisted on sleeping in a separate bedroom, apart from her current husband. Some ministers, dissatisfied with such separate sleeping arrangements, seek to break up new marriages entirely. I will argue below that such teachers have seriously misinterpreted Jesus' teaching. Indeed, they create new divorces, thereby directly undermining the same teachings they accuse others of undermining!

Adultery against One's Spouse

Jesus warned, "Anyone who divorces his wife and marries another woman commits adultery against her" (Mark 10:11). We should note first the final words, "against her." Such divorce is not a victimless crime; Jesus declares that this action is wrong because it wrongs an innocent party. In his culture, a wife could be divorced for almost any reason, and she had little economic recourse once divorced. This compounded the offense of the divorce.[7] Yet the heart of the offense would be true in any culture: to break faith with one's spouse is wrong.

Clearly Jesus is against divorce. He is against divorce because it violates a covenant; can wound the innocent; and is bad for spouses, children, society, and ourselves.[8] Jesus is not, however, against those who have *suffered* divorce, and he is specifically defending, at least in Mark 10, those who are divorced against their will.[9] With many other scholars, I would argue that, while Jesus uses a graphic rhetorical form to communicate his point, the point is to prohibit breaking one's marriage, not to require permanent singleness for those already divorced.[10]

But what does the Lord mean by "commits adultery"? When Jesus' predecessors and contemporaries used the expression literally, it meant sleeping with another man's wife.[11] If Jesus speaks literally, his calling remarriage adulterous can mean only one thing: he is claiming that in God's sight one or both members of the remarrying couple remain married to their original spouse. Every act of intercourse would therefore be adultery, and every moment of emotional intimacy would be emotional unfaithfulness to the first spouse.

Even more troubling, if all marriage is indissoluble in God's sight, then even the innocent party remains bound to the marriage. This is explicit in Luke 16:18: "Anyone who divorces his wife and marries another woman commits adultery, and the man who marries a divorced woman commits adultery."

The Character of Jesus' Saying

Did Jesus mean this saying literally? In view of the rest of Jesus' teaching on the subject, the case is much stronger that he was using hyperbole, i.e., rhetorical overstatement.[12]

Five observations support the likelihood that Jesus meant this saying hyperbolically. First, Jesus regularly used hyperbole and other graphic rhetorical devices. Ancient speakers commonly used hyperbole, and Jewish sages used it, especially in memorable sayings like this one.[13] One cannot read many of Jesus' sayings and doubt that he often spoke this way. Can a camel really fit through a needle's eye (Mark 10:25)? Did Pharisees really gulp down camels whole (Matt. 23:24)? How often did Jesus' followers move literal mountains (Mark 11:23)? Although I believe that the church should take Jesus' teachings about possessions far more seriously than we do, most Christians regard as hyperbole the command to give absolutely everything (Luke 12:33; 14:33), and many early Christians observed the principle without impoverishing themselves (Acts 2:44–45; 12:12–13; cf. Luke 3:11). That Jesus often used hyperbole does not *prove* the fact he was doing so here, but it should silence objections that claim it unlikely.

Second, the very context of the divorce saying in Matthew 5:32 is hyperbole.[14] Jesus not only calls remarriage "adultery" in 5:32; he calls lust "adultery" in 5:28. If we are ever tempted to break up subsequent marriages as acts of "adultery" based on 5:32, we ought to take equally seriously Jesus' remedy for the "adultery" of lust in 5:29–30: "If your right eye causes you to sin, gouge it out and throw it away.... And if your right hand causes you to sin, cut it off and throw it away." Certainly Jesus provides a graphic warning against the danger of eternal destruction if we continue in marital unfaithfulness, whether by lust or (more conclusively) by breaking up a marriage; but few interpreters in history have taken Jesus' solution for the former as literally as his solution for the latter.[15]

Third, and more significantly, Jesus' other teachings in fact assume the dissolubility of marriage. When I say "dissolubility," I do not mean that Jesus elsewhere permitted us to divorce; he taught against it.[16] But I mean that Jesus elsewhere contradicts the notion that marriage is ontologically indissoluble, i.e., that in God's sight one remains married to one's original spouse (the grounds for making remarriage adulterous).

Jesus does not say to the woman at the well, "You were married once and have lived with five men since then." Rather, he says, "You were married five times but are just living with someone now" (John 4:18).[17] Some interpreters may counter that Jesus was speaking figuratively to this woman rather than in his saying about remarriage.

It is, therefore, important to note that the very context of the saying with which we began, Mark 10:11–12, recognizes that marriage is ontologically dissoluble. "Therefore," Jesus warns, "what God has joined together, *let* no one separate" (10:9 TNIV, emphasis added). There is little point in forbidding a separation that cannot occur in any case. Jesus forbids it because it *can* but *should not* occur. The image of remarriage as adulterous (presented hyperbolically, as if marriage is indissoluble) serves the same rhetorical function: preserve your marriage. It is demand, not a cosmic law claiming that marriage remains intact no matter what.[18]

Fourth, Matthew twice specifies an exception for the innocent party (Matt. 5:32; 19:9).[19] Jesus prohibits divorce here *except* for the cause of unfaithfulness (*porneia*). The meaning of *porneia* has been much debated, but it should be read as any sort of sexual infidelity against the marriage. It is a basic rule of biblical interpretation not to overspecify the meaning of a term; while *porneia* can include incest, premarital sex, or extramarital sex, it is a broader term that, when left unqualified, includes any kind of sexual immorality. There is no contextual reason to suppose a narrower interpretation here, and for that reason more scholars favor the infidelity interpretation than any other single position.[20] "Except for infidelity" makes good sense in a context that discusses interpretations of the law: in all ancient law, infidelity was a standard legal charge affecting a divorce settlement.[21]

This interpretation perfectly fits the context of Matthew 19:9. In Matthew 19:3, the Pharisees ask Jesus about the lawful grounds for divorce. In Jesus' day, two schools of Pharisaic thought debated this very question: Does Deuteronomy 24 allow husbands to divorce their wives for any reason (so the school of Hillel), or only for marital unfaithfulness (so the school of Shammai)?[22] Jesus sides with the latter (Shammaite) school of interpretation, though his hyperbole states the matter far more strongly than any Shammaite would: not only is divorcing a faithful spouse wrong, but such a divorce is invalid in God's sight. Jesus establishes his case by appealing to God's original purpose for marriage in Genesis 2:24; in the new kingdom ethic, obeying God's ideal takes precedence over concessions to human weakness in a civil law (Matt. 19:4–8).[23] This appeal prohibits disciples from breaking up their marriages; but does it address those whose marriages are broken against their will?

The issue in question in the hyperbolic image of remarriage as adultery is whether the person remains married to his or her original spouse in God's sight. Therefore, Jesus' allowance of divorce in case of the spouse's unfaithfulness must permit the innocent party to remarry subsequently, since the divorce is valid and the person is no longer married to the adulterous spouse. No (monogamist) laws permitted remarriage without a valid divorce; conversely, a valid divorce by definition (often explicit in divorce deeds) *constituted* freedom to remarry.[24]

But while the point of the exception clause is to relieve the betrayed party from being mistreated by the church, it also has implications for the other party and for how we should interpret the saying. If the innocent partner is no longer married to the guilty party in God's sight, how can the guilty party still be married to the innocent one?[25] That the text does not need to raise the question reinforces the point: while the exception for infidelity is meant to free the innocent party, the saying is meant simply to prevent divorce, not to make an ontological statement about its indissolubility.

Fifth, Paul, an inspired interpreter of Jesus' saying, recognizes another exception.[26] He acknowledges that Jesus warns the believer not to divorce or abandon a faithful spouse (1 Cor. 7:10–11). But Jesus did not specifically address the situation of a spouse leaving the believer, a situation Paul envisions in religiously mixed marriages in 1 Corinthians 7:12–15. So Paul qualifies Jesus' teaching for this situation.[27]

Qualifying a general principle for a situation not specifically envisioned in the principle in no way meant dishonoring the principle.[28] Jewish sages often offered sayings like proverbs that were general principles requiring qualification in some situations, and most people in antiquity understood the need to interpret such sayings accordingly.[29] They did so even for legal principles[30] and the brief kinds of statements concluding public arguments[31] (such as Mark 10:9 or Matt. 19:9). Such general principles could conflict among themselves if applied beyond the situation to which they most clearly applied.[32] Just as Jesus qualifies earlier Scripture without rejecting it (Matt. 5:22, 28, 32, 34, 39, 44), Paul quotes Jesus and then adds his own wisdom (1 Cor. 7:10–12), which he believes is from the Spirit (7:40).

Paul notes that if the unbeliever (not bound by Jesus' teaching) leaves the believer, the believer is "not under bondage" (7:15). This is the exact language in ancient divorce contracts for freedom to remarry, and one could not expect his words to mean anything else in this context.[33] Why does Paul feel free to apply Jesus' words this way? Probably because he understood the character of Jesus' teaching better than most of us do today. He recognized the hyperbolic element in the image and understood that Jesus' prohibition of divorce was a general principle to which there might be exceptions.

Paul probably intends this assumption also in 1 Corinthians 7:27–28.[34] Although he addresses "virgins" in this context (v. 25), he distinguishes those freed from marriage in verse 27 from virgins (v. 28).[35] He is merely digressing to offer a comparison with his previous words in verse 15. One who is bound to a wife (i.e., married)[36] should not seek to be freed (i.e., divorced), nor should one who has been "freed" (lit.; not simply "free," i.e., "unmarried" more generally, as in the NIV) seek marriage. If "freed" means divorced in the first line of verse 27, it must at least include divorce in the second line. But Paul goes on to affirm that those who do remarry have not sinned (v. 28); this is identical to the counsel Paul offers virgins (vv. 25–26, 28).

WHICH EXCEPTIONS?

Probably four of the six divorce texts in the NT (Matt. 5:32; 19:9; 1 Cor. 7:15, 27–28) make exceptions for an innocent party. Some wish to explain away the four exceptions that explicitly qualify the principle (stated more baldly in Mark 10:11–12; Luke 16:18). By this hermeneutic, however, one could never use other texts to qualify those containing general principles, even though it is plainly necessary, for example, in proverbs (a form influential in the teachings of Jesus and other Jewish sages). Consider these two examples:

- A lazy person becomes poor, and a diligent person becomes rich (see Prov. 10:4; cf. 14:24); yet it is better to be poor and righteous than rich and wicked (see Prov. 28:6; cf. 16:8)
- We should answer a fool according to his folly, lest he think himself wise (Prov. 26:5); but we should not answer a fool according to his folly, lest we be like him (Prov. 26:4).

So shall we answer or not answer a fool?[37] By placing the two proverbs side by side, the book of Proverbs invites us to carefully consider how to apply each one.

Similarly, when addressing the demands of discipleship, Jesus tells us to "hate" our parents (Luke 14:26); yet in a different situation he requires us to love and honor them to the point of supporting them (Mark 7:9–12). And again, Jesus declares that those who call others "fools" will be damned (Matt. 5:22); yet he himself calls religious hypocrites "fools" (Matt. 23:17). Examples could be multiplied, but these should be sufficient to make the point. Refusing to qualify general principles by other principles would make nonsense of much of our Bible.

The two explicit biblical exceptions, adultery and abandonment, share a common factor: they are acts committed by a partner against the obedient believer. That is, the believer is not breaking up his or her marriage but is confronted with a marriage covenant already broken.[38]

OTHER EXCEPTIONS?

Could there be other exceptions? Not if we must be able to *quote* a specific saying of Paul before we declare one—but there may be some if we follow his *example*. Granted, we are not writing sacred Scripture as he was, but Paul did not know that his letter to the Corinthians would become part of the canon (he could not be sure that the Lord would tarry that long), only that he surely had the Spirit's leading (1 Cor. 7:40).

If Paul had to reapply Jesus' teaching in a new way for a situation Jesus did not directly address, we may be called on to do the same. This is, in fact, an essential factor in how we approach the Bible: we must hear and obey its point, not just quote its words. Otherwise we can address only a limited range of issues the Bible specifically addresses, and not countless others that we must argue from biblical principles. The Bible says little or nothing *specifically* about abortion, the abolition of slavery, drug abuse, pornography, domestic abuse, and many other pressing issues, yet most of us believe that it holds serious implications for these issues. Dare we "freeze" its message in ancient history and simply quote it to cover all of our needs? Or must we read it dynamically as God's Word to the first readers in their situations, which he intends for us to reapply in analogous ways when we face different situations?[39]

Consider how Jesus and the Pharisees clashed over divorce. Both quoted biblical texts, but Jesus looked for the principle that revealed God's ideal purpose. The Pharisees emphasized the wording of the law without sufficient regard for the very people the law was meant to help, because their "hearts were hard" (TNIV; just as Moses used the law's wording to accommodate their hard hearts [cf. Mark 10:5]). Jesus consistently looked past the specific formulations of commands in the law to the heart of the law (e.g., Matt. 5:17–48).[40] Most Christians today do not regard all laws in their OT form as binding on Christians, but we learn from their principles.

On a practical level, the question of other exceptions is a pressing one. This would be true even if the only reason were one for which marriage is important to single people who have never been married. If Paul advises that marriage is a spiritually helpful solution to the dangers of passion (1 Cor. 7:9),[41] should we think that divorced Christians, many of whom have tasted marital intimacy, are necessarily less tempted by passion than unmarried single Christians who (ideally) have never tasted it? I do not intend this observation as a moral argument justifying all remarriage (some might exploit such a "reducing temptation" argument to justify any sort of behavior roundly condemned by Scripture), but as a pastoral argument highlighting the importance of considering the question of other exceptions.

Yet our exceptions to Jesus' rule against divorce should be consistent with the character of the exceptions in the NT: the believer is not free to break up the marriage but only to accept that the unrepentant partner has irreparably broken it. As Southern Baptist ethicist David Gushee notes, "One cannot find a biblical text in which burning a child or a wife on the arm with a cigarette (or throwing them down the stairs or banging their heads against the wall or enlisting them in a murder plot) is listed as grounds for divorce. Such actions, however, constitute a fundamental assault on the meaning of the marriage covenant."[42] Given the usual pattern of physical abuse (in which the abusive spouse periodically apologizes or excuses the behavior but, without commitment to serious counseling, does not change), I believe that God would hold us responsible to accept a pattern of abuse as grounds for divorce and thus, on the argument above, also for remarriage.[43]

But some pastoral situations invite us to define "abuse." Few church leaders today would protest at least temporary separation when a husband is beating a wife and her life or physical safety is in danger. But is beating where we draw the line? A disabled man once confided to me that his wife lived off his disability, yet she was leaving him uncared for, hoping to get his inheritance as soon as he died. She was not beating him, but was he in any less danger?

Facing Some More Difficult Questions

At the opposite extreme, few would accept as "abuse" the sort of harsh words that are, sadly, all too common in marital arguments. Yet between harsh words and physical abuse lie a variety of difficult situations. What of a woman whose husband's incessant verbal assaults have reduced her to the point of contemplating suicide? This is not physical abuse, but most would at least expect separation and counseling in the hope of helping the couple survive. Still, anyone can claim "abuse," and people who simply want to end their marriages often offer such claims. How do we evaluate the genuineness or extent of abuse? Likewise, granted that our goal is preserving marriages, when does the counselor accept one partner's intransigence as irreversible (at least on a pessimistic reading of 1 Cor. 7:16)?

My specific role as a biblical scholar does not qualify me to deal with questions beyond the clear biblical cases, and the claims become much more complicated beyond physical abuse. Some circumstances do indeed appear analogous to biblical exceptions, but I fear writing words that some would use as an "easy out" in a difficult marriage. Yet, unlike many scholars, pastors and other church leaders cannot escape such questions, which confront us in our practice of ministry. Otherwise we may simply turn a blind eye to sinful behavior that is already affecting marriages in our congregations. (Continuing to be an associate pastor in a church and to teach pastors in a seminary that is oriented toward practical ministry helps keep me in touch with the sorts of concrete, real-life concerns I had to grapple with as a pastor, though full-time pastors face these concerns on a much more regular basis than I do.)

I think of several women whose husbands were drug addicts. One, who resisted the thought of divorce for years because she loved her husband, finally divorced him after he had stolen and sold everything they had, causing them to lose their home. Another cared little about her house but divorced her husband after he beat her in front of their child. Another remained faithful over the years, but her husband exploited the situation to get their children hooked on drugs. I don't have all the answers, but as the writer in this book assigned to defend additional exceptions, I have the responsibility at least to ask the question, are these cases "abuse"? Asking it more controversially, if these marriages end, must these women remain permanently unmarried?

If a member of my congregation, broken by such suffering in years past, is now able to enter a healthy marriage, will I agree to perform the remarriage ceremony, or will I refuse to participate? When I grapple with such questions, I remember the way

Jesus treated the broken. And while I'm trying to decide the case, I also remember how Jesus treated "righteous" people like me, who felt the need to judge everyone's case: "They [teachers of the law and Pharisees] tie up heavy, cumbersome loads and put them on other people's shoulders, but they themselves are not willing to lift a finger to move them" (Matt. 23:4 TNIV). And perhaps, "If you had known what these words mean, 'I desire mercy, not sacrifice,' you would not have condemned the innocent" (Matt. 12:7). Or even, "Whoever causes one of these little ones who believe in me to stumble, it would have been better for him ... to be cast into the sea" (Matt. 18:6, my translation). Such verses do not tell us where to draw the line; they do, however, raise the stakes if we draw it too strictly.

Some evangelicals go further, citing examples like "sexual abandonment" as grounds for divorce. I am reticent to count "neglect" and sexual deprivation as permission for divorce (though they demand counseling); despite the value of marital relations for controlling temptation, Paul does not include sexual deprivation in grounds for divorce, even though he mentions both subjects in the same context (cf. 1 Cor. 7:2–6, 10–16). I do believe that the sacrifices of preserving the marriage bond are worth enduring as long as there remains hope of saving the marriage. Yet some evangelical biblical scholars and pastoral counselors have argued that deliberate sexual "abandonment" does sever the marriage covenant (a "one flesh" union defined in part by physical intimacy, except when this is physically impossible).[44] Ideally, this book could represent their position as a fourth, beyond my own, hence representing a broader evangelical spectrum.

Extreme Examples

Although I am reluctant to go so far, extreme examples give me pause. A young man in another country confided that his wife had refused the slightest touch and nearly all conversation since they married. I could neither confirm nor deny his claim that her refusal was unprovoked and that she had never been abused. In his country (as in the Bible), arranged marriages are common, so his knowledge of her before the marriage was likely less substantial than is common here. But now he wanted advice. She was refusing to divorce him because she believed it was wrong, but she was urging him to divorce her; he was sure they needed to divorce, as reluctant as he was to be divorced.

Was her alleged behavior analogous to unfaithfulness? I was reluctant to stand before God someday, having offered advice either unhealthily strict (like Paul's opponents in Galatia) or too lenient (like many of the Corinthian Christians). Like others this husband had consulted, I had to admit I did not have an easy answer beyond what was explicit in Scripture. I had no access to the wife or opportunity for counseling; I had one hour with this man and might never see him again. Yet I offered what little I could.

"I cannot keep loving her!" he pleaded.

"If you cannot love her for her sake, can you try to keep loving her for now for Jesus' sake?" I suggested.

During the next year, we would pray for a miraculous breakthrough in his marriage. For Jesus' sake, he said, he was willing to do that. Some readers of this book will think me too lenient for not simply rebuking his consideration of divorce; others will think me too harsh for not endorsing the burial of an apparently dead union. Not having the answer myself, I merely pose the question for you to consider.

I like writing Bible commentaries that deal with objective, concrete information; where I lack that, I usually take refuge in the biblical scholar's freedom to say, "I don't know." But in real-life pastoral situations, we sometimes have to make decisions (even if it is sometimes simply the decision *not* to make one), regardless of whether we know all the answers. Biblical scholars help keep pastoral counselors anchored to the text's demands, but pastoral counselors also stretch us to consider situations that our articulation of those demands has not addressed.

The lack of absolute certainty on where best to draw the line in some cases is an admitted problem of my position, one I feel keenly. Yet this is often a problem when we must move from explaining the original meaning of biblical passages to applying them to unexpected situations today. I suspect that Jesus did not intend to tell us where to draw the line so much as to make us faithful to our marriages. The exceptions were for marriages broken against our will; I wish these exceptions were much rarer than they are today.

REMARRIAGE WITHOUT EXCEPTIONS?

Let us for a moment imagine that we could always determine the innocent party (in divorces where there is one) and never faced ambiguous cases. Even in such an unlikely scenario, we still face the practical question of the guilty party. After the publication of ... *And Marries Another*, a man called me in anguish. He admitted that he had been the guilty party in his divorce many years earlier; after the divorce, he remarried, started a new and happy family, and over the years had several children. Convicted by the Lord for how he had treated his first wife, however, he genuinely repented of the divorce and sought to make restitution. Then he discovered that his former wife, who had never remarried, was praying for his return. He had noticed that I had not addressed his situation in my book, and he wanted the Bible's guidance. I had not wanted to confuse the clear biblical case for exceptions by introducing less clear issues in the book. But now a Christian needed an answer.

Certainly we should consider certain factors before allowing remarriage. For emotional reasons, even an innocent party is wise not to remarry immediately; remarriages right after divorces usually lead to new divorces. Dysfunctionalities must be corrected, and wounds and insecurities healed; this is even more the case for a clearly guilty party, who may well repeat the same behavior in a subsequent marriage. Further, it is biblically appropriate for a clearly guilty party (such as an adulterer or abuser) to be placed under some form of church discipline until he or she has offered clear signs of repentance and made restitution as best as is possible. Given the various venues available for weddings, we cannot stop a premature or morally wrong marriage from taking place; but we can speak truth in love, which will likely be remembered a few years hence when troubles inevitably come.

Paul warned believers who (against his instructions) divorced committed spouses that they should either remain single or return to their spouses (1 Cor. 7:10–11).[45] This is consistent with our understanding of Jesus' divorce saying articulated above, because reconciliation remains possible if neither partner has remarried. The focus, in other words, is still on preserving (or, in this case, restoring) marriage rather than on treating a remarriage as adultery.

But what happens once the other spouse remarries, making reconciliation (the likely point of 1 Cor. 7:11) impossible? Or when the person divorced before his or her conversion, hence before understanding Jesus' teaching the way a believer should? Or what if the believer ignores this passage and simply remarries? I am loathe to imagine a genuine believer disobeying Paul's teaching; but if, God forbid, a person claiming to be a believer divorces without adequate cause and remarries, do we seek to preserve the new marriage or to separate it as an act of adultery? (This is a question separate from the matter of church discipline.)[46] Because I am convinced that Jesus' saying about remarriage being adultery was hyperbole, I believe that its point was (as in all other NT teachings on divorce) to prevent the dissolution of marriage, not to prevent remarriage per se. Therefore, I conclude that we need not consider breaking up subsequent marriages, whether or not we would have approved of the divorce.

"PERMITTING" REMARRIAGE

From my perspective, the chapter's question requires a further clarification: What do we mean by "permitting" remarriage? If we mean approving of the divorce that preceded the remarriage, there are many evangelical scholars who would feel more comfortable with a wider range of exceptions than I do. Like my fellow contributors to this book, I am fairly conservative in resisting divorce, at least by the standards of how the North American church lives. But the book's subject is about *remarriage* after divorce, not about divorce per se.

A second way to approach the question, therefore, would be, "Under what circumstances would I sanction a remarriage?" Certainly the biblical texts pose no problem for me with regard to the innocent party. Thus, were the question simply, "Would you *ever* sanction a remarriage?" the biblical text would protect me from anxiety in my task. Yet such a question may be closer to the lot that has fallen to my friend Bill Heth. I offered my best answer to the hardest question under "Remarriage without Exceptions?" above: I believe that genuine, demonstrated repentance is efficacious when reconciliation (the best form of restitution) has become impossible. This seems clear at least in the case of one who divorced before becoming a Christian; though the divorce may have been a sin, it was probably not a deliberate revolt against the teaching of the one the person calls Lord.

But there is a third approach that seems to me to be closer to the heart of this book's question, one that the texts in question force on churches with remarried but repentant members who were not specifically "innocent parties." In light of the biblical texts about divorce, I understand the real question of "permitting remarriage" in terms of accepting a remarriage as a valid marriage in God's sight once it is done. Are we called to break up second marriages as acts of adultery? I would argue that we are called to value them as genuine marriages and thus to nurture them and seek to prevent further divorce. Treating the subsequent marriage as a valid one, we should recognize that two wrongs (a second divorce) will not create a right.

REMARRIED PERSONS IN CHURCH LEADERSHIP

Those who prohibit remarried (or often even single divorced) people from ministry most often appeal to 1 Timothy 3:2, sometimes translated as "husband of but one wife" (lit., "one-woman man"). That "one wife" is addressed specifically to divorce, however, is hardly self-evident. Some cultures apply the text to prohibit polygamy; Eastern Orthodox tradition cites it against remarriage after a priest's wife's death.

The phrase parallels one used for widows in 1 Timothy 5:9, where it echoes a phrase used in many inscriptions to praise faithful wives whose husbands had no reason to divorce them. That verse's context probably rules out a prohibition of remarriage (5:14). In ancient Ephesus, a "one-woman man" as a criterion for church leadership likely referred to marital faithfulness, in contrast to the use of concubines or the widespread practice of extramarital affairs.[47] While this standard is important anywhere, it certainly must have borne repeating in Ephesus, where (in addition to immorality being rife in the broader society) some strict false teachers were prohibiting marriage altogether (1 Tim. 4:3).

The wife of one young minister left him for her friend's husband. He fought the divorce for two years, the maximum his state allowed, hoping to convince her to return, but she refused. Thereafter he was barred from ministry in many circles for years—not because anyone doubted that he was the innocent party but, as some leaders put it, to "maintain a standard."[48] (The standard evidently was, "It is not enough to be godly; you must also be able to control your spouse's choices." One wonders what this says for both Hosea and God himself in the Old Testament.) Ironically, when this man finally remarried fourteen years later, the discrimination stopped.

Indeed, we must apply a standard, but applying it to a victim rather than to a perpetrator is like punishing a rape victim because we oppose rape. In God's sight, condemning the righteous is no less sinful than justifying the guilty (cf. Exod. 23:7; Prov. 17:15). Some churches also have a double standard. I have, unfortunately, known cases where pastors abandoned their spouses for other partners; the abandoned wife often became a pariah in her own church and was sometimes treated (especially by those loyal to their pastor) as being responsible for the breakup of her marriage.

What of a person who broke up a marriage twenty years ago, was afterward converted, and has lived a godly life since then? Should we exclude him or her from leadership any more than we would exclude a former murderer (like Saul of Tarsus or Moses) who has demonstrated repentance and maturation in the faith? Does it fit biblical principles to treat this sin as less amenable to cleansing by our Lord's blood than any other?

SUMMARIZING THE CASE

I have argued that divorce is permissible for adultery, abandonment, and abuse (not, of course, for such contemporary claims as "incompatibility" or "growing apart"). I have also argued that the primary point of Jesus' teaching is the exclusion of divorce, so we should recognize later remarriages as legitimate marriages (i.e., we should not seek to break them up), whether or not we concur with the grounds for the divorce. This is not to deny the propriety of exercising church discipline in the case of a clearly invalid divorce, but to suggest that two wrongs (i.e., the breaking up of a subsequent union) do not make a right.

A RESPONSE TO CRAIG S. KEENER

Gordon J. Wenham

I have met Craig Keener only once—very briefly at a conference—so the following comments may be quite misguided, but both his book and his article give me the impression that he is very strongly motivated by pastoral concern for divorced persons who remarry. This is admirable. We are instructed to "carry each other's burdens, and in this way ... fulfill the law of Christ" (Gal. 6:2). Those who have suffered the terrible emotional trauma of divorce need all the compassion and support the church can muster. So I share Craig's revulsion at the crassness of some who have applied the New Testament teaching on divorce with insensitivity and harshness. My father was once asked about the recipe for successful ministry. He replied, "90 percent tact!" Preeminently, in the realm of broken relationships, immense wisdom and tact are needed. Unfortunately, Craig seems to have experienced too many situations where grace was not present.

THE NO-REMARRIAGE VIEW NEED NOT LEAD TO INSENSITIVITY

The mistaken application of a sound principle does not invalidate the principle. Those who believe that no-remarriage views inevitably lead to pastoral insensitivity should read Andrew Cornes, *Divorce and Remarriage*, or the more popular Johann Christoph Arnold, *Sex, God and Marriage*.[1] These writers demonstrate that strong principle and compassion are not opposite poles; but just as our Lord dealt compassionately with the adulterous woman without condoning her sin (John 8:1–11), so the modern church can handle the complex issues thrown up by divorce and remarriage in a sensitive and loving way.

In my response to Craig, I propose to say more about the pastoral implications of his views than about his biblical arguments, as many of these I've already covered in my response to Bill.

THE BIBLICAL TEXTS

I begin with the biblical texts. I agree with Craig that the exception clauses in Matthew cannot be restricted to adultery. *Porneia* ("sexual immorality") covers a wide range of sexual sin, which in ancient times may have required the divorce of the guilty party. However, I do not believe that Jesus thereby gave the right to remarry. With the apostle Paul (1 Cor. 7:11) and Bill Heth (see his chapter), I think that Jesus hoped for forgiveness and reconciliation in such a situation. The point is that Jesus recognized there were circumstances in which society required divorce, and in this situation Jesus did not call the divorcer an adulterer, but neither did he grant the right to remarry. We can well envisage other situations today where separation is required because of the spouse's behavior, and this would be a legitimate extension of the *porneia* exception. However, if remarriage is not envisaged, and Jesus' demand that we should forgive those who sin against us is taken seriously, separation would become a last resort.

For the most part, I find Craig's exegetical arguments rather weak. He draws in various verses from 1 Corinthians 7 that have no relevance to the issue, while ignoring the obvious text of Romans 7:2–3. Frequently he argues that divorce entails the right to remarry, a view I have tried to refute in my essay and in my response to Bill. But at the same time Craig admits that divorce for the wrong reason is invalid in God's sight, which is to allow that a divorce may be legal yet ineffective. It apparently entitles a person to remarry without in fact terminating the first marriage, so that any subsequent union is termed adulterous. This is an important concession to the no-remarriage view.

Craig argues that Jesus' statement, "anyone who divorces his wife and marries another woman commits adultery against her" (Mark 10:11), is hyperbole because it cannot be taken literally. There is no doubt Jesus loved colorful speech and used vivid imagery to make his teaching memorable. So how can we distinguish hyperbole from literal language? I would suggest three tests. First, we assume that Jesus' words are to be taken literally unless there are indications to the contrary; a literal interpretation is thus our default reading. We cannot take literally camels going through the eye of a needle or suppose that Pharisees could swallow them, so we conclude that these remarks are hyperbole; but there is nothing to tell us that remarriage after divorce could not be viewed as adultery. You only have to suppose that the speaker views the first union as still binding on both parties to take it literally.

The second test is one of genre: does the remark sound like a wild prophetic image, or like a sober law? Anyone who reads Exodus 21–23 will find numerous laws formulated like Mark 10:11 (e.g., Exod. 21:13–17). So this again points to the statement's literalness. Laws are to be taken literally. Finally, the context suggests the same. In Mark 10 the disciples are asking for an explanation of his harsh dismissal of the Pharisees' views on divorce. They wanted a straightforward explanation, not a riddle. Clearly the early church found no difficulty in taking Jesus literally, so I do not see why the modern church should either.

WRESTLING WITH PASTORAL ISSUES

I now turn to some of the pastoral issues Craig raises. He begins with cases where pastors have attempted to break up second marriages. I have never advocated this. My view is that people should be discouraged from remarrying after divorce; but where such marriages exist, it would be tactless in the extreme to suggest that the couple break up. The OT gives many examples of how to react to difficult ethical situations (e.g., bigamy); clearly, bigamy was not God's intention, for he gave Adam only one wife (Gen. 2:22). Subsequent stories about bigamists (e.g., Gen. 4:19–24; chs. 29–50) show that their family lives were complicated, but there is no suggestion that Jacob, for instance, should throw Leah out. Bigamy was tolerated in OT times despite its problems, and it seems to me that the church today has to tolerate couples who have remarried while at the same time discouraging others from going that way. It is a task that demands immense tact and wisdom.

Toward the end of his chapter, Craig presents many heartbreaking cases where first marriages have broken up. He asks whether we can deny the victims of such tragedies the chance to find happiness in a second marriage, especially where the victim is not responsible for the divorce. Of course, our instinct is to say, "Yes, they must be allowed another chance." But I think we need to pause to reflect before we give a spontaneous yes to such pleas for remarriage. We should consider how difficult it is in many cases to know who is responsible for the first marriage's failure. Bill Heth gives an example from his experience as to how he was taken in, and Craig acknowledges this in passing. Then there is the question of what happens if the second marriage breaks up, as it is statistically more likely to do. Do we allow a third marriage, or a fourth, or a ...? What happens to a doctrine of lifelong marriage if the principle of remarriage is freely conceded?

Craig focuses on the plight of the divorced person who would like to remarry. But we must not be so individualistic in our ethics. We must think of the effect of such a decision on others. Children of divorced people are very upset by divorce, but even more by remarriage; it destroys their last hope that their parents will be reconciled. The divorcée who does not find a new partner is aggrieved when her former husband remarries, especially where they all belong to the same church.

There are also the wider costs to society—not simply the huge welfare costs of supporting single parents and their children, but the way in which our whole social fabric is undermined by the destabilization of marriage. The whole idea of commitment and honor is undermined when promises made before God "to have and to hold from this day forward, for better, for worse, for richer, for poorer, in sickness and in health, to love and to cherish, till death do us part" may be set aside and then repeated to someone else.

Hard cases make bad laws. We see this in the abortion debate. Heartrending cases are used to justify the principle of abortion, and then the door is opened for abortion on demand.

The same is true once the principle of remarriage is conceded. So although it may seem very unkind if a church refuses to marry a divorced person, in the longer term it is, I believe, for the good of our society. Such a policy will benefit children. It will encourage couples who have difficulties in their marriages to work at them. It will give the watching world a glimpse of God's undying love. But to implement this policy in today's society will be extremely difficult. It demands conviction, wisdom, tact, and prayer. I pray that you, the reader of this book, will be given grace to know how to proceed in your situation and that you will have the strength to carry it out.

A RESPONSE TO CRAIG S. KEENER

William A. Heth

As one might suspect, since I occupy the middle position in this book, I am drawn to each of the other two views to varying degrees. I found a kindred spirit when I first came across Gordon Wenham's writings on divorce and remarriage back in the early 1980s, and I credit Craig Keener's 1991 book with planting the seeds that have led me to where I am today. On the one hand, I fear that some remarriages after divorce may be prohibited where Jesus and Paul might have permitted them; on the other hand, I fear that an increase in divorces and remarriages may occur for inadequate or insignificant reasons. However, since I believe that Craig takes the tragedy of broken marriages as seriously as anyone—probably even more seriously—I know that nothing he writes would ever intentionally open up the door to more divorces and remarriages.

MY FORMER VIEW

Craig's work, in fact, alerted me to a major problem with my former view. Where there is a truly innocent offended party in divorce (I know this is difficult to determine in many cases), do Jesus' divorce sayings expressly require permanent singleness for divorced persons? Craig made it clear that he felt this was both unjust and unmerciful. I had to agree that Jesus' heart would go out to those who have suffered divorce. I could see that Craig was not just making human happiness via remarriage the determinative criterion of what God would sanction. It seems that only if marriage is indissoluble this side of a spouse's death, and any remarriage an offense against the Creator God, would Jesus deliberately seek to prohibit innocent victims of divorce from ever marrying again.

Craig begins by pressing the question, what is the outcome if we take Jesus' sayings about divorce and remarriage in their most literal sense? Simply put, Jesus would be saying that everyone who remarries after any divorce commits adultery (Mark 10:11–12; Luke 16:18). If this is the case, then marriage must be indissoluble. If marriages are indissoluble, then remarried couples are living in adultery; i.e., every time they have marital relations, they are committing adultery. Since no one who habitually sins makes it into heaven (1 Cor. 6:9–10; my addition to Craig's points), either remarried couples must refrain from marital relations (separation from bed and board), as the church father Jerome required, or pastors should seek to break up second marriages.

Craig sends a wake-up call to Christians who claim to read and apply the Bible at face value. Not only does common sense tell us that something is wrong with this picture, but Craig notes that we should have expected writers like Paul to address such concerns, but he does not. Further, Craig notes that there is ample evidence that Jesus commonly used hyperbole or rhetorical overstatement. Thus, we are in agreement on the point that Jesus' divorce sayings may well employ preacher's rhetoric to condemn strongly the abuses he saw around him.

AGREEMENT AND DISAGREEMENT

There is really very little with which I disagree in Craig's chapter. We both make the point that Jesus' statement, "What God has joined together, let no one separate" (Mark 10:9 TNIV), does not mean that the marriage covenant *cannot* be broken but that it *should not* be. We both agree that Scripture recognizes subsequent remarriages as valid marriages. Craig underlines Jesus' testimony to this based on what Jesus says to the woman at the well (John 4:18). I have made this point over the years in correspondence based on Paul's teaching in 1 Corinthians 6:9–11. "Adulterers" are included in the list of sins about which Paul says, "And that is what some of you were. But you were washed, you were sanctified, you were justified in the name of the Lord Jesus Christ and by the Spirit of our God." It seems likely that one or more of the new Corinthian believers had been adulterers before they were converted. It is also likely that some were already divorced and remarried when they became believers. Nevertheless, Paul can say, "and that is what some of you were." The apostle did not think of remarried believers as adulterers or those living in a continual state of adultery. His remarks also implicitly connect a believer's standing in God's sight with his or her repentance (cf. 1 Cor. 1:2; 2 Cor. 7:9, 10; 12:21; 1 Thess. 1:9). Craig and I both agree that 1 Corinthians 7:15 is further evidence that Paul did not understand Jesus' divorce sayings as exceptionless absolutes.

However, I still cannot find permission for divorced persons to remarry in Paul's counsel in 1 Corinthians 7:27–28. The ESV now helps clarify Paul's intent: "Are you bound to a wife? Do not seek to be free. Are you free from a wife? Do not seek a wife. But if you do marry, you have not sinned, and if *a betrothed woman* marries, she has not sinned" (emphasis added). There is a growing consensus, though it's a view not without its problems, that Paul is speaking to the concerns of some engaged couples in verses 25–38 (cf. NIV, NRSV, RSV on vv. 36–38). The men were asking Paul whether or not to follow through with their promise to marry in view of the ascetic teaching they had come under in Corinth (7:1b). Paul's initial (vv. 25–28) and final (vv. 36–38) remarks in this section are directed specifically to these couples. Though Paul personally prefers the single state, he wants them to know—contrary to what the ascetics probably taught—that it is *not* sinful to go through with their plans to marry (vv. 28, 36). Thus, I doubt that 1 Corinthians 7:27–28 contributes much to discussions of NT teachings on the ethics of remarriage after divorce.

What about additional exceptions beyond the two based on Matthew 19:9 and 1 Corinthians 7:15? Craig says, "If Paul had to reapply Jesus' teaching in a new way for a situation Jesus did not directly address, we may be called on to do the same" (p. 111). The guiding premise for deciding which other exceptions qualify is consistency with the other two exceptions: "the believer is not free to break up the marriage but only to accept that the unrepentant partner has irreparably broken it" (p. 112).

Within this framework, Craig argues that a pattern of physical abuse would qualify as an additional exception and considers other potentially analogous situations.

Given that I also believe Paul made an exception for a new situation not directly addressed by Jesus, and that "staying married" means fulfilling the covenant obligations expressed in one's marriage vows, I cannot deny that a repeated pattern of physical abuse would be a violation of the marriage covenant. This is the antithesis of caring for and cherishing one's wife (Eph. 5:29). David Instone-Brewer's work may point a way to ground this scripturally. He identifies two additional biblical grounds for divorce based on Exodus 21:10–11, a text stating that a husband must give a wife food, clothing, and marital love/duty. Rabbinic sources classified these under two headings: material neglect (cf. 1 Cor. 7:32–35) and emotional neglect (cf. 1 Cor. 7:1–9). Instone-Brewer argues that both the rabbis and Paul applied these obligations equally to the wife and the husband. Not only that, but he shows how the three provisions of Exodus 21:10–11 became the basis for vows in Jewish marriage contracts and can also be found in the Christian marriage ceremony based on references to them in Ephesians 5:28–29. Since in Matthew 19 and Mark 10, Jesus was asked only about where he stood on the Deuteronomy 24:1 debated ground, he did not necessarily exclude the other recognized grounds. Thus, Instone-Brewer defends four grounds for permitting divorce and remarriage after marriage vows have been violated, extensive forgiveness has been extended in the hope that genuine repentance will follow (Luke 17:3–4), and yet the vow-breaker stubbornly refuses to repent of his or her actions. He believes that Hosea's example shows that God finally ended the relationship only when it was totally destroyed. All of this is plausible but for me is not yet a conviction.

WHERE TO DRAW THE LINE

I admire Craig's willingness to tackle the tough questions and the way he forthrightly challenges his readers with the very real dilemmas spouses face in tragic marriage situations. Craig admits that knowing "where to draw the line" is a problem for his position (p. 115). I can see that it is beginning to be a problem for mine as well; indeed, it will be for all who do not believe that marriage is inherently indissoluble; who hold that Paul, led by the Spirit, applied Jesus' divorce sayings to a new situation; and who believe there are comparable breaches of the marriage covenant today that need to be pastorally addressed—situations where, for all practical purposes, the restoration of the marriage is impossible. On the one hand, I have suggested that the offended, repeatedly sinned-against spouse is the one who should be the one to say when "enough is enough," and he or she might decide this too soon; on the other hand, I see the need for prayerful church leaders to come alongside, to guide, and to help financially support truly victimized spouses reticent to remove themselves from tragic situations because they *know* that God hates divorce.

Chapter 3: Remarriage for Adultery, Desertion, or Abuse

1. Craig S. Keener, *... And Marries Another: Divorce and Remarriage in the Teaching of the New Testament* (Peabody, Mass.: Hendrickson, 1991).

2. Craig S. Keener, *A Commentary on the Gospel of Matthew* (Grand Rapids: Eerdmans, 1999), 189–92, 462–72.

3. Craig S. Keener, *1–2 Corinthians* (NCBC; Cambridge: Cambridge Univ. Press, 2005), 64–67, 70.

4. In an earlier book, Bill and Gordon characterized the view that allows remarriage after adultery as "the evangelical consensus"; it was the dominant view of the Reformers. Although Roman Catholic tradition historically has opposed remarriage (despite the disagreement of some Catholic biblical scholars), the Eastern tradition allows remarriage for some divorced persons (cf. Anthony C. Thiselton, *The First Epistle to the Corinthians* [NIGTC; Grand Rapids: Eerdmans, 2000], 542).

5. When I refer to "innocent" in this essay, I mean those who did not break their marriage covenant, not, as the position has been caricatured, perfect spouses (a title that applies to God and Christ alone).

6. See Keener, *... And Marries Another*, 50–52.

7. Other Jewish teachers also recognized that by making divorce more difficult, they would protect the woman (e.g., *t. Ketub.* 12:1).

8. See documentation for its dangers in David P. Gushee, *Getting Marriage Right* (Grand Rapids: Baker, 2004), 21–83.

9. See Myrna and Robert Kysar, *The Asundered: Biblical Teachings on Divorce and Remarriage* (Atlanta: John Knox, 1978), 43; R. T. France, *Matthew* (TNTC; Grand Rapids: Eerdmans, 1985), 280; Margaret Davies, *Matthew* (Readings; Sheffield: JSOT Press, 1993), 54; if one pressed the saying literally rather than as hyperbole, however, it would have the opposite effect (cf. Rudolf Schnackenburg, "Matthew's Gospel as a Test Case for Hermeneutical Reflection," in *Treasures New and Old: Recent Contributions to Matthean Studies*, ed. D. R. Bauer and M. A. Powell [Atlanta: Scholars Press, 1996], 253). Klyne R. Snodgrass ("Matthew and the Law," in *Treasures New and Old*, 118) argues that Jesus agrees with the purpose of OT laws, some of which forbade (Deut. 22:19, 29) and others of which required (Exod. 21:11; Deut. 21:14) divorce, both to protect the wife.

10. See, e.g., W. D. Davies and Dale Allison, *A Critical and Exegetical Commentary on the Gospel According to Saint Matthew* (ICC; Edinburgh: T&T Clark 1988), 1:532; France, *Matthew*, 106; cf. M. J. Down, "The Sayings of Jesus about Marriage and Divorce," *ExpTim* 95 (1984): 332–34; Mark J. Molldrem, "A Hermeneutic of Pastoral Care and the Law/Gospel Paradigm Applied to the Divorce Texts of Scripture," *Int* 45 (1991): 43–54; David Parker, "The Early Traditions of Jesus' Sayings on Divorce," *Theology* 96 (1993): 372–83.

11. By applying the requirement to both genders, Jesus implicitly prohibits polygamy as well—but this was rare in Jewish Palestine and illegal in the Greek and Roman world.

12. For this view, see, e.g., Robert H. Stein, *The Method and Message of Jesus' Teachings* (Philadelphia: Westminster, 1978), 8–12; Stein, "Is It Lawful

for a Man to Divorce His Wife?" *JETS* 22 (1979): 119; Stein, "Divorce," 192–99, in *Dictionary of Jesus and the Gospels*, ed. J. B. Green and S. McKnight (Downers Grove, Ill.: InterVarsity, 1992), 198; James M. Efird, *Marriage and Divorce: What the Bible Says* (Nashville: Abingdon, 1985), 57–59; Keener, ... *And Marries Another*, 12–25.

13. See, e.g., *m. ʾAbot* 2:8; *ʾAbot R. Nat.* 36A; Aristotle, *Rhet.* 3.11.15, 1413a; *Rhet. Her.* 4.33.44; Quintilian, *Inst.* 8.6.73–76.

14. See discussion in Keener, *Matthew*, 182–89; and in ... *And Marries Another*, 12–20.

15. One alleged exception, Origen, who is said to have castrated himself, incurred the church's censure.

16. The point of calling a saying "hyperbole" is not so we can dismiss it by claiming, "That is 'just' hyperbole." The point of hyperbole is to grip our attention.

17. For discussion, see Craig S. Keener, *The Gospel of John: A Commentary* (Peabody, Mass.: Hendrickson, 2003), 1:606–8.

18. Cf. esp. David R. Catchpole, *The Quest for Q* (Edinburgh: T&T Clark, 1993), 238.

19. See fuller discussion in Keener, *Matthew*, 189–92, 462–72; and in ... *And Marries Another*, 21–49.

20. See documentation in Keener, *Matthew*, 466–69; ... *And Marries Another*, 28–37. If any narrowing is possibly suggested in the context, it is adultery (because the original couple is married).

21. See, e.g., S. Safrai, "Home and Family," in *The Jewish People in the First Century*, ed. S. Safrai and M. Stern (Philadelphia: Fortress: 1974–76), 2:790; John J. O'Rourke, "Roman Law and the Early Church," in *The Catacombs and the Colosseum*, ed. S. Benko and J. J. O'Rourke (Valley Forge, Pa.: Judson, 1971), 182; Keener, *Matthew*, 91.

22. Especially *m. Giṭ.* 9:10; *Sifre Deut.* 269.1.1; cf. also *m. Ketub.* 7:6. On this issue (unlike some others), the more liberal Hillelite view was dominant (Sir. 25:26; Philo, *Spec. Laws* 3.30; Josephus, *Ant.* 4.253; *Life* 415, 426). The Shammaite position is a little broader than "adultery," apparently including obvious immodesty (viewed as attempted seduction). This might be one reason Jesus uses *porneia* rather than *moicheia* here (though *porneia* sometimes represents marital infidelity in the LXX, e.g., Jer. 2:20; 3:2, 9; Ezek. 16:15; Hos. 2:2, 4, 6; Amos 7:17; Sir. 23:23).

23. Qumran texts (CD 4.20–5:2; 11QT 56.18–19) use the same text to prohibit royal polygamy, not (against some interpreters who read Jesus' teaching into Qumran) divorce (see Keener, ... *And Marries Another*, 40–41). "Concession" was an established legal category in Jewish law (see David Daube, "Concessions to Sinfulness in Jewish Law," *JJS* 10 [1959]: 1–13).

24. In addition to the term's lexical meaning, note ancient usage, e.g., in *m. Giṭ.* 2:1; 9:3; *CPJ* 2:10–12, §144. If "except for infidelity" modifies Jesus' statement about divorce rather than remarriage, as some (esp. Gordon Wenham and William Heth) have argued, it does so precisely because, in Jesus' graphic statement, it is the validity of the divorce that is in question.

25. Indeed, if remarriage is "adulterous," then an abandoning spouse's remarriage would de facto constitute a qualifying case of *porneia* (cf. 1 Cor. 7:15)! Matt. 5:32 specifies only the divorced wife and whoever marries her as involved in adultery; this, however, fits the hyperbolic image in a Palestinian-Jewish setting where only the husband had a normal right to divorce (cf. Keener, ... *And Marries Another*, 35, 47–48, 51; Burton Scott Easton, "Divorce in the New Testament," *AThR* 22 [1940]: 78–87, esp. 82; Robert A. Guelich, *The Sermon on the Mount: A Foundation for Understanding* [Waco, Tex.: Word, 1982], 200–201).

26. See fuller discussion in Keener, ... *And Marries Another*, 50–66, esp. 53–56.

27. Also recognized by others, e.g., Craig L. Blomberg, *Matthew* (NAC 22; Nashville: Broadman, 1992), 111–12; Geza Vermes, *The Religion of Jesus the Jew* (Minneapolis: Augsburg, 1993), 34 n. 34.

28. Other principles in Jesus' teaching, such as not condemning the innocent (Matt. 12:7) or the principle of mercy (Matt. 23:23), may have invited qualifying the saying as well.

29. See Keener, ... *And Marries Another*, 22–25; cf. Robert C. Tannehill, *The Sword of His Mouth* (SBL Semeia Supplements 1; Missoula, Mont.: Scholars Press, 1975), 95–98; Stein, *Method and Message*, 11. Maxims and proverbs, general statements of principle requiring qualification (cf., e.g., Prov. 18:22 with 11:22; 12:4; 21:9; see other examples below), also appear in Greek and Roman sources (e.g., Isocrates, *Demon.* 12, *Or.* 1; Aristotle, *Rhet.* 2.21.1–2, 12–15, 1394a–95b; *Rhet. Her.* 4.17.24–25; Petronius, *Sat.* 4; Plutarch, *Poetry* 14; *Mor.* 35EF).

30. E.g., Quintilian, *Inst.* 7.6.1, 5; frequently in rabbinic texts.

31. Cf., e.g., Plutarch, *Ages.* 21.4–5; *Statecraft* 7; *Mor.* 803CD; *Sayings of Spartan Women*, passim; Diogenes Laertius 1.35; 2.72; 6.2.51.

32. E.g., Prov. 26:4–5; Publilius Syrus 162–63 with 178; 211 with 212.

33. See, e.g., *m. Giṭ.* 9:3; *CPJ* 2:10–12, §144; P. Grenf. 2.76.10–11; for rabbinic sources, see esp. the excellent work by David Instone-Brewer, *Divorce and Remarriage in the Bible: The Social and Literary Context* (Grand Rapids: Eerdmans, 2002).

34. See fuller discussion in Keener, ... *And Marries Another*, 63–64.

35. Some interpret "wife" (v. 27) in view of the later discussion of (probably) betrothals (vv. 36–38); but (1) that is an issue Paul explicitly raises only after this context; (2) Paul uses "wife" in the preceding context only for marriage; and (3) morally speaking, Paul would not assume that a betrothed Christian must be readily distinguishable from a "virgin" in verse 28 (cf. also v. 36, where the betrothed is the latter).

36. As noted, the term Paul uses for "wife" in v. 27 is also his usual one, not to be confused with his different term for a betrothed virgin afterward.

37. See other examples in Craig Keener, *The IVP Bible Background Commentary: New Testament* (Downers Grove, Ill.: InterVarsity, 1993), 235.

38. Blomberg (*Matthew*, 293) rightly points out that exceptions beyond those stated in Scripture must be governed by the principle that unites the

two biblical exceptions: (1) both infidelity and abandonment destroy central components of marriage; (2) both leave an innocent party unable to save the marriage; (3) both use divorce only "as a last resort." He is aware that some will abuse this freedom, but we cannot for that reason punish the innocent party who genuinely needs it.

39. For example, when Paul instructs slaves to submit to slaveholders (Eph. 6:5–8), we understand that, while the principle of submission is universal, Paul is not sanctioning the institution of slavery itself. See, e.g., discussion in Craig S. Keener and Glenn Usry, *Defending Black Faith: Answers to Tough Questions About African-American Christianity* (Downers Grove, Ill.: InterVarsity, 1997), 36–41.

40. Cf. my comments in *Matthew*, 180–82.

41. See Keener, … *And Marries Another*, 67–82. Some apply Matt. 19:10–12 only to divorced persons, but in view of the immediate flow of context, it addresses the disciples' concern about initial marriage if it cannot be escaped (see fuller discussion in my *Matthew*, 470–72).

42. Gushee, *Getting Marriage Right*, 81.

43. Chrysostom (*Hom. 1 Cor.* 19.4) applied 1 Cor. 7:15 to abuse as well as to abandonment. Although Christians must face suffering, God does not require us to remain in it unnecessarily (cf. Matt. 10:23; Mark 13:14; Acts 14:6).

44. Certainly intercourse is critical to the marriage covenant as at least its initial consummation; see Gordon P. Hugenberger, *Marriage as a Covenant: Biblical Law and Ethics as Developed from Malachi* (Biblical Studies Library; Grand Rapids: Baker, 1998), 216–79; cf. 1 Cor. 6:16. Cf. further discussion of exceptions in David Instone-Brewer, *Divorce and Remarriage in the Church: Biblical Solutions for Pastoral Realities* (London: Paternoster, 2003), 82–93.

45. The sometimes-cited case of Michal was technically different, since (apart from political considerations) David had never legally divorced her (2 Sam. 3:14–16; cf. Deut 24:4; 1 Sam. 25:44).

46. Discipline is appropriate if we can be certain that the abandonment was unjustifiable—though it is better to err on the side of mercy if we cannot be certain. Certainly all literal adultery, including all divorcing for the purpose of marrying another, is properly subject to church discipline until repentance is forthcoming.

47. For the full argument, see my … *And Marries Another*, 83–103. Immorality was also a problem in Crete (Titus 1:6; see Bruce W. Winter, *Roman Wives, Roman Widows: The Appearance of New Women and the Pauline Communities* [Grand Rapids: Eerdmans, 2003], 163).

48. See my "The Almost-Unpardonable Sin: Is Divorce Treated as a Justice Issue in Your Ministry?" in *Building Unity in the Church of the New Millennium*, ed. Dwight Perry (Chicago: Moody Press, 2002), 329–33; … *And Marries Another*, 6–10; esp. "Blaming the Victim?" *Moody Monthly* (November 2002): 40, 42; "Divorce as a Justice Issue," *Prism* 5 (1998): 6–8, 20.

Chapter 3: A Response to Craig S. Keener
(Gordon J. Wenham)

1. Andrew Cornes, *Divorce and Remarriage: Biblical Principle and Pastoral Practice* (paperback; Inverness: Christian Focus, 2002); Johann Christoph Arnold, *Sex, God and Marriage* (Farmington, Pa.: Plough, 1996).

CONCLUSION:
THREE KEY QUESTIONS FOR YOU
TO ANSWER

Mark L. Strauss

We have reached the end of our journey. I'm sure you have profited from the positive, pastoral, and constructive tone of all three authors. I hope you've come away with a better understanding of the biblical teaching on this critically important topic.

As you continue to wrestle with this subject personally or pastorally, let me summarize some key issues and questions raised in this book. All the authors agree that divorce is a tragedy in the church and in society, causing great emotional and spiritual damage to individuals and families. Divorce is contrary to God's will for human relationships, and Jesus' strong words against it should never be minimized. God's purpose for his people is to have healthy, monogamous, lifelong marriages where each spouse seeks the best in the other person.

All the authors also agree that when conflicts arise, couples should seek every means possible to reconcile their differences. Christian marriages are intended to be a reflection of God's covenant relationship with his people and to reveal to the world the reconciling power of the gospel. If Christians cannot work through their differences and live together in love and unity, how can we presume to tell the world that we have the answer to life's problems?

THE ROLE OF THE CHURCH AND ITS LEADERS

The church needs to develop a stronger focus on keeping marriages together, not just on spending its energy debating the grounds for divorce and remarriage. Church leaders have often been too quick to ostracize those who are divorced and too slow to provide the resources necessary to maintain healthy marriages. Preventive maintenance is essential for every relationship. Churches should provide premarital counseling for engaged couples to help prepare them for the inevitable conflicts they'll face. Older couples who have weathered life's storms should seek out relationships with younger ones, sharing their wisdom on how to make marriage work. Sermons should regularly focus on how to maintain healthy relationships, and marriage enrichment seminars should be a regular part of the church calendar.

While the church must work proactively to prevent divorce, the reality is that we are all sinful people and that divorce happens. Sometimes one partner may be primarily at fault, acting selfishly, irresponsibly, or immorally to cause irreparable damage to the relationship. Other times, the fault may be more evenly divided. But in every case, sin is the ultimate cause of broken relationships. Jesus said that God permitted divorce "because your hearts were hard" (Matt. 19:8).

FORMING YOUR OWN CONCLUSIONS: THE THREE KEY QUESTIONS

So what does the Bible teach about remarriage after divorce? The conclusions you reach will depend on your answers to three key questions.

The first centers around what Jesus meant by the so-called "exception clause" of Matthew 5:32 and 19:9 ("except for sexual immorality," TNIV). There is no doubt that the Old Testament permitted (though did not encourage) divorce and remarriage and that all rabbis of Jesus' day considered adultery a legitimate grounds for divorce and remarriage. It is also clear that Jesus reacted strongly against the permissive attitude of some rabbis, pointing to the seriousness of the marriage covenant and warning that remarriage after divorce constituted adultery (Mark 10:2–9; Luke 16:18). But was this a general (and hyperbolic) statement that needed qualification (so Heth and Keener), or was it the establishment of a firm principle (so Wenham)? The former see Matthew's exception clause as qualifying Jesus' strong statement—an allowance for remarriage in the case of adultery; the latter sees it not as an exception but as a clarification of the principle: a husband cannot be said to have made his wife commit adultery (by divorcing her, resulting in her remarriage) if she had *already* committed adultery during the marriage. Put another way, did Jesus agree with his contemporaries that adultery was an acceptable ground for remarriage, or did he challenge that assumption and overrule the rabbinic teaching of his day?

A second key question has to do with the meaning of Paul's statement in 1 Corinthians 7:15 that a person "is not bound" following the desertion of an unbelieving spouse. All the contributors to this book agree that Paul spoke strongly against divorce and encouraged divorced persons to remain single in the hope of reconciliation with their partners (1 Cor. 7:11). But again, was this a firm principle (so Wenham), or was it open to exception (so Heth and Keener)? The latter see Paul's statement "is not bound" as parallel to the language of Jewish divorce statements, meaning "you are free to remarry"; the former sees it merely as the recognition of the reality of the desertion, not as permission to remarry—meaning "you are no longer required to live with that person in a marital relationship."

The third key question asks whether these two "grounds" for remarriage (adultery and desertion) constitute God's full revelation on the subject (so Heth, with some openness to other grounds), or whether they are representative—i.e., examples of the kinds of situations that constitute grounds for remarriage (so Keener, with due caution for the potential abuse of these principles). Stated another way, may we draw general principles from these two grounds that could be applied to other situations, or should we limit grounds to those explicitly set out in Scripture?

SOME PRACTICAL CONCERNS

If you are a pastor or Christian leader who seeks greater insight into this issue, I encourage you to reread the chapters that espouse views different from your own. All of us have blind spots in our life, and growth comes through hearing God's Spirit speak through his Word—sometimes in ways we least expect. Each person who deals with this subject, either pastorally or personally, should approach it with a humble and teachable spirit, fully aware that we are all sinners in need of God's grace and forgiveness and that none of us have the last word on this difficult issue. Our knowledge and insight will remain partial and incomplete until we see Christ face-to-face (1 Cor. 13:12). Expressing respect, tolerance, and love for those who disagree with us is essential if we are to maintain the unity of faith that God demands for his church (Eph. 4:3; Phil. 2:1–2; Col. 3:14).

If you are divorced and contemplating remarriage, let me encourage you to spend significant time in prayer and in seeking godly counsel from people you respect for their spiritual wisdom and insight. I hope you will also take time to consider the circumstances that led to your divorce, asking yourself how you have grown and matured since that experience. Marriage is not necessarily the key to spiritual fulfillment and happiness. Singleness and celibacy are celebrated in Scripture as means to greater intimacy and devotion to the Lord (1 Cor. 7:32–35) and should be viewed as a viable option for all believers. God gives many people the gift of singleness, and he is more than sufficient to meet your needs through the presence of his Spirit and through deep, meaningful relationships with other believers. The church must work harder to make single and divorced people feel welcome in their congregations and to remove the stigma so often associated with those who are unmarried.

If you decide, through prayer and study, that remarriage is an option, I hope you will ask yourself several probing questions: Am I harboring deep resentment and bitterness toward my former spouse? Am I unwilling to forgive that person for the wrongs he or she has committed against me? Do I find myself justifying past actions and shifting the blame to others? If you answer yes to one or more of these questions, it's a warning sign that you have deeper issues that should be resolved before moving into a new relationship. I would encourage you to seek guidance from your pastor or from a counseling professional before going forward. Moving too quickly into another relationship to escape loneliness or to meet physical or emotional needs can have disastrous results, where you may find yourself repeating the tragedies of your past.

If you are wrestling with guilt from the brokenness of a former relationship, I want to remind you that there are no unpardonable sins in the Christian life. God offers healing and forgiveness to all who come to him in humility and repentance and acknowledge their sins. He can restore and renew the wounded and brokenhearted. For our part, God calls us to forgive those who have hurt us and to seek reconciliation with them. He wants us to make amends and to ask forgiveness from those we have hurt, as we live all of our relationships with Philippians 2:3–4 in mind: "Do nothing out of selfish ambition or vain conceit, but in humility consider others better than yourselves. Each of you should look not only to your own interests, but also to the interests of others." God's purpose for you is to love and worship your heavenly Father and to love others as yourself. As we learn to put these foundational commands into action, we will be on our way to experiencing fulfilled and meaningful relationships that will last a lifetime.

May God richly bless you as you seek to honor him in all your relationships and as you grow in the grace and knowledge of our Lord Jesus Christ.

RESOURCES FOR FURTHER STUDY

Blomberg, Craig L. "Marriage, Divorce, Remarriage, and Celibacy: An Exegesis of Matthew 19:3–12." *Trinity Journal* 11 NS (1990): 161–96.

Clark, Stephen. *Putting Asunder: Divorce and Remarriage in Biblical and Pastoral Perspective.* Bryntirion, Bridgend, Wales: Bryntirion Press, 1999.

Collins, Raymond F. *Divorce in the New Testament.* Collegeville, Minn.: Liturgical Press, 1992.

Cornes, Andrew. *Divorce and Remarriage.* London: Hodder & Stoughton, 1993.

Deasley, Alex R. G. *Marriage and Divorce in the Bible and the Church.* Kansas City, Mo.: Beacon Hill, 2000.

Efird, James M. *Marriage and Divorce: What the Bible Says.* Nashville: Abingdon, 1985.

Heth, William A., and Gordon J. Wenham. *Jesus and Divorce: Towards an Evangelical Understanding of New Testament Teaching.* 3rd ed. Carlisle: Paternoster, 2002.

Heth, William A. "Jesus on Divorce: How My Mind Has Changed." *Southern Baptist Journal of Theology* 6 (Spring 2002): 4–29.

House, H. Wayne, ed. *Divorce and Remarriage: Four Christian Views.* Downers Grove, Ill.: InterVarsity, 1990.

Hugenberger, Gordon P. *Marriage as a Covenant: Biblical Law and Ethics as Developed from Malachi.* Biblical Studies Library. Grand Rapids: Baker, 1998; Leiden: Brill, 1994.

Instone-Brewer, David. *Divorce and Remarriage in the Bible: The Social and Literary Context.* Grand Rapids: Eerdmans, 2002.

_____. *Divorce and Remarriage in the 1st and 21st Century.* Cambridge: Grove, 2001.

144 | Remarriage after Divorce in Today's Church

Keener, Craig S. ... *And Marries Another: Divorce and Remarriage in the Teaching of the New Testament*. Peabody, Mass.: Hendrickson, 1991.

Liaboe, G. P. "The Place of Wife Battering in Considering Divorce." *Journal of Psychology and Theology* 13 (1985): 129–38.

Murray, John. *Divorce*. Phillipsburg, N.J.: Presbyterian & Reformed, 1953.

Stein, R. H. "Divorce" in *Dictionary of Jesus and the Gospels*. Edited by J. B. Green and S. McKnight. Downers Grove, Ill.: InterVarsity, 1992.

ABOUT THE CONTRIBUTORS

Gordon J. Wenham is senior professor of Old Testament at Cheltenham and Gloucester College of Higher Education in Cheltenham, England. A recognized expert on the Pentateuch, he has written commentaries on Genesis, Leviticus, and Numbers, in addition to publishing numerous studies in the Old Testament. He coauthored *Jesus and Divorce* with William A. Heth and has written many books of his own, including *Story as Torah: Reading Old Testament Narrative Ethically; Exploring the Old Testament: A Guide to the Pentateuch;* and *The Book of Leviticus* in Eerdmans' New International Commentary on the Old Testament series.

William A. Heth resides in Upland, Indiana, where he has been professor of New Testament and Greek at Taylor University since 1987. He received his master's and doctoral degrees in New Testament literature and exegesis from Dallas Theological Seminary in Dallas, Texas. He is the coauthor, with Gordon Wenham, of *Jesus and Divorce.*

Craig S. Keener is professor of biblical studies at Palmer Theological Seminary (formerly Eastern Baptist Seminary) in Wynnewood, Pennsylvania. He is also an associate minister at Enon Tabernacle Baptist Church in Philadelphia. He is the author or coauthor of fourteen books, including six New Testament commentaries. Three of his commentaries have won *Christianity Today* book awards. He received his Ph.D. in New Testament and Christian Origins from Duke University.

Mark L. Strauss is professor of New Testament at Bethel Seminary in San Diego, where he has taught since 1993. Previously he taught at Biola University, Christian Heritage College, and Talbot School of Theology, and he has served on the staffs of several churches. His books include *The Davidic Messiah in*

Luke-Acts and *Distorting Scripture? The Challenge of Bible Transla-tion and Gender Accuracy*. He wrote the volume "Luke" in the Zondervan Illustrated Bible Backgrounds Commentary series, coauthored "Mark" in the revised Expositor's Bible Commentary (forthcoming), and wrote the volume "Mark" in the Zondervan Exegetical Commentary series (forthcoming). He received his doctorate from the University of Aberdeen.

Paul E. Engle, series editor for Counterpoints: Church Life, served for twenty-two years in pastoral ministry on the East Coast and in the Midwest and has been an adjunct teacher in several seminaries, teaching homiletics and doctor of ministry classes. He holds the M.Div. degree from Wheaton College Graduate School and the D. Min. degree from Westminster Theological Seminary. Paul is the author of eight books, including *Baker's Wedding Handbook*, *Baker's Funeral Handbook*, and *Baker's Worship Handbook*. He serves as associate publisher for editorial development and as executive editor at Zondervan.

DISCUSSION AND REFLECTION QUESTIONS

CHAPTER 1: NO REMARRIAGE AFTER DIVORCE

1. What do you see as the strongest and weakest arguments for believing that the New Testament disapproves of remarriage after divorce? Why?
2. Can you give some specific examples of these arguments?
3. How can the church both affirm Jesus' standards for marriage and declare the forgiveness of sins?
4. Is it helpful to distinguish between tolerating an action and approving it? Why or why not?
5. Should higher standards of behavior be expected of church leaders than of laypeople? If so, why? If not, why not?
6. What can be done to make more marriages last? What advice would you give to young couples contemplating marriage? What advice would you give to the leaders of your church?
7. What changes in marriage discipline would you like to see in your church? Why? If you are content with the way things are at present, can you identify some reasons for your satisfaction?

CHAPTER 2: REMARRIAGE FOR ADULTERY OR DESERTION

1. Though this chapter argues that the marriage covenant is "dissolvable" or "breakable," do you think there is scriptural evidence that would suggest otherwise? Which, if

any, of the attempts in this chapter to harmonize Matthew's report of Jesus' teaching with Mark and Luke's exceptionless report make the most sense to you?

2. What are the pros and cons of using first-century sociocultural background information found outside the Bible to help "fill in the gaps" for twenty-first-century readers who try to hear and understand the biblical text just the way a first-century reader would?

3. If sexual unfaithfulness throughout the history of human marriage is such a grave offense against the marriage covenant, what makes it possible for a spouse to forgive an unfaithful partner who genuinely repents of his or her sin? What circumstances would indicate that one has waited long enough for a spouse to repent?

4. What are the implications of Paul's telling those who divorce for invalid grounds to remain unmarried or else be reconciled (1 Cor. 7:10–11), while at the same time telling widows and widowers who cannot control their sexual desires that they should remarry (1 Cor. 7:8–9)? How would Paul counsel married couples who, for one reason or another, are physically unable to engage in marital relations?

5. How would you define "all reasonable attempts to save the marriage" when one's marriage covenant has been violated by a serious sexual sin or desertion? What role should church leaders play in coming alongside innocent victims of divorce, either to assure them that their marriage is irretrievably broken or to encourage them to hold on a bit longer in the hope of repentance and reconciliation?

6. If you are currently married, consider your relationship as a couple in the context of your larger family, church, community, work, and world. What do you need to continue to do, stop doing, or start doing to solidify the covenant loyalty you pledged to one another on your wedding day?

7. As a follower of Jesus today, how would you try to convey to your peers what Jesus taught about divorce and remarriage? How should the church encourage spouses

to keep their vows when marriages encounter threats of dissolution?

CHAPTER 3: REMARRIAGE FOR ADULTERY, DESERTION, OR ABUSE

1. For what grounds does the Bible explicitly permit divorce? What do these grounds have in common?
2. What other situations do you think are genuinely analogous to these kinds of exceptions?
3. Granted that there are exceptions, how do we work to prevent divorce? What principles in Jesus' teaching prevent us from excusing inappropriate divorce?
4. Why is it wrong to break up second marriages, even if the grounds for divorce were wrong?
5. How should we treat those who acted unjustly in breaking up their marriages yet have repented and done their best to make restitution?

SCRIPTURE INDEX

SUBJECT INDEX

158 | Remarriage after Divorce in Today's Church